Linda,
Such a
pleasure
to know
you!

NETWORKING:

Naked & Unafraid

Second Edition

Kathryn Crawford Wheat

WILSHER
PUBLISHING

Wilsher Publishing
Box 5055
Katy, Texas • 77491

WilsherPublishing.com
A Division of Wilsher Media Group

Networking: Naked & Unafraid
Second Edition

ISBN: 978-1-59930-437-3

Cover and layout design created by:
Ashlee Wilsher
AshleeWilsher.com

A Special Thanks

There are many extraordinary people in my life that have played instrumental roles in helping this book become a reality and they deserve special thanks. First, there are all those networkers that I observed and learned from. Without you, this book wouldn't have been possible. Special mention goes to the late Lee Farb, a super networker. I hope he knew how much his support and probing questions helped me grow. Hank Moore, my birthday twin, the REAL Houston Legend who was so kind to write the foreword for this book; having your endorsement means the world to me! I'm so delighted to have met you out there in the networking world! Mom, the unconditional love and strength you've demonstrated in your own life has shaped and molded me into the woman I am today. You are beautiful and amazing! Ronny, your encouragement and unfailing belief in me got me started on this crazy journey and your positivity has kept me going even when I wanted to quit. Without you, I never would have dared to dream that I was capable of so many of the things that I do today. Cindy, you've seen me through so much. Over the years we've been through many life-changing moments and I can't wait to see what the future holds. Ashlee, your talent is truly a gift! You are a design genius and I'm honored to have worked with you. I especially appreciate all the evenings you gave me after a full day of work to get this book cover and design done. Jacob, you are a patient man. Thanks for putting up with me taking Ashlee away from you all those evenings. Weston and Katie, you are brilliant, talented, incredible and capable of anything you set your mind to. You inspire me every day and I'm proud to be your mom.

What People are Saying

Thank you again for your class. You have a special gift for crowd participation and I learned much more today than I have learned in the last year from networking.
~ Steven S.

You knocked it out of the park! Thank you for your speech at our Chamber meeting.
~ Chris B.

This information is so practical and much needed in the business world. Any additional classes you do I would love to attend.
~ Tiffany L.

I am new to networking and I found your speech so helpful. I wanted to hear more! You're a mix of comedy, inspiration, motivation and education. ... can't beat that!
~ Brandie S.

Kathryn, I can't thank you enough! God makes no mistakes and has a purpose for uniting individuals. My reason for meeting you is crystal clear. In my most humble form I sincerely thank you for planting the seed of encouragement within me. Your kind words, clear vision and networking tools have been so essential to me. When we first met you made me think outside the box and dragged me out of my comfort zone. I was once told by a dear friend that successful women help lift others as they themselves climb ... You Kathryn Crawford Wheat are amazing!
~ Yasira S.

You are causing a ripple effect to others. God bless you!

~ Lynne C.

Thank you for a fabulous class yesterday. I walked away with many ahaa moments!

~ Kristi S.

Thank you so much for your class. You really have been a hit with our Sales Counselors.

~ Angelina S.

I am rarely inspired, but you were inspiring!

~ Robert G.

I want to thank you again for the wonderful job you did yesterday. I am excited about having your group do more classes with us in the future. I am going to implement what I learned from you yesterday!

~ Jeanne M.

The richest people
in the world look for
and build networks,
everyone else looks
for work.

~ *Robert Kiyosaki*

Preface

It's not who knows of you, it's whom you have an authentic relationship with that really matters! That's the real question. The reason we network is to build mutually beneficial relationships that can expand our circle of influence. Any successful leader, executive, entrepreneur, salesperson, or even politician will tell you how important their network is to them.

Successful networking builds an association of people who provide us with advice, knowledge, emotional support, and business opportunities. It involves surrounding yourself with like-minded, positive business professionals and experts in your field who will share their expertise and experience with you. You can think of your network like a valued support team. There is a wealth of knowledge out there waiting for you to tap in to!

Contents

SECTION 1:

STRIP DOWN

SECTION 2:

GET NAKED & UNAFRAID

SECTION 3:

DON'T BE AFRAID: YOU ARE READY!

SECTION 4:
YOU'VE SHOWN UP NAKED ALL OVER TOWN

Foreword

Hank Moore
Futurist - Corporate Strategist™

Business is at a crossroads. The rules have changed...always have and always will. A great many mosaics make up The Big Picture. Yet the wider perspective in business is rarely seen.

This book is about widening the scope much further. Whenever we review what made relationships and business successful, we see that Big Picture thinking occurred. The potentiality of people and organizations is a progressive journey from information to insight to knowledge.

I endorse this book and its author, Kathryn C. Wheat. I've known and worked with some of the greatest women in the world. They included Eleanor Roosevelt, Audrey Hepburn, Lady Bird Johnson, Lucille Ball, Lyndall Wortham, Barbara Jordan, Ima Hogg, Claire Booth Luce, etc. I put Kathryn C. Wheat on that rarified list.

Kathryn has impacted me because of her warmth, sincerity, know-how, determination and the ability to make you seem to be the most important person in the room, the society and the world.

We share a special bond, the same birthday (October 9). We are wired similarly: a kinship toward caring, sharing, community service and the bigger picture of life. Our fellow October 9th birthday celebrant John Lennon said it eloquently: "There's nothing you can see that isn't shown. Nothing you can know that isn't known. You can learn how to be you in time. Love is all you need."

Networking can be a grand series of experiences. Where many have their hands out, Kathryn has her heart out. She brings charm and grace to human dynamics. When she inspires us all to do well and achieve, by golly we do it.

That's the essence of this humanity-focused book. It had its genesis with the Woman's InSite magazine, the heartfelt blogs about humanity in the business world and the networking events. It has been articulated in Kathryn's speeches and in her impact on others.

Much of the wisdom to succeed lies within. People under-perform because they are not given sufficient direction, nurturing, standards of accountability, recognition and encouragement to out-distance themselves. Organizations start to crumble when their people quit on each other.

Healthy organizations absorb all the knowledge and insight they can, embracing change, continuous quality improvement and planned growth. The level of achievement by a company is commensurate to the level and quality of its vision, goals and tactics. The higher its integrity and character, the higher its people must aspire.

This book and its author, Kathryn C. Wheat, embrace the heart and soul of business. Chapters are written in such a way as to be interpreted on several levels. Part common sense and part deep wisdom, they are intended to widen your focus and inspire the visionary that exists within you, the reader. Futuristic ideas can and should become your ideas, mindset and ethical business practice.

Kathryn says that she is an average person who is trying to make a difference. I say that she is an exemplary role model, with advice and insights well worth hearing and taking to heart. I say that she brings out the greatness in us.

In being her most encouraging best, she mentors you to be your best. Kathryn's book includes inspiring words for a lightning rod of change, progression and the future.

Hank Moore, Futurist - Corporate Strategist™
Author of:

- *The Business Tree* Published by major New York imprint, plus seven international editions
- *Houston Legends*
- *The High Cost of Doing Nothing - Why good businesses go bad*
- *The Classic Television Reference*
- *Power Stars to Light the Flame... The Business Visionaries and You*
- *American Business Legends*
- *The Future Has Moved... and Left No Forwarding Address*
- *The $50,000 Business Makeover*
- Two editions of the *Chicken Soup* books
- Harvard Business Review Monograph Series
- Library of Congress Archive Series
- Strategy Driven Business Monograph Series

"Only those who
will risk going too far
can possibly find out
how far one can go."

~ T.S. Eliot

Introduction

The Fast Track to Remarkable Networking

Imagine attending a very popular networking event hosted at a wine bar jam-packed with business people talking, smiling and exuding confidence. It appears that everyone has met each other before and you are the only newbie who doesn't know the secret handshake. You must somehow break the ice and start talking to people about your business. This was me several years ago as I ventured out into the networking world, naive and inexperienced. I couldn't even differentiate who was at the bar to network and who was hanging out having a drink with friends!

I had no idea how to walk up to a total stranger in a business setting and simply introduce myself. So many questions swam through my head. Should I hand them my card and move on or do I linger and chat? If I talk to them, what do I say? What do we talk about? What if there's an awkward silence? What if they start talking about something I don't understand? Should I get a drink first? Do I have pepper in my teeth? I wanted to run!

I finally zeroed in on two ladies who were sitting at the bar. They looked like they were friendly enough. What's the worst thing that could happen, right? I gathered my courage, plastered a big smile on my face and thrust my hand toward them and said, "Hi, I'm Kathryn Wheat." They both looked at me like I was an idiot! I could tell they were barely holding back laughter. Panic immediately set in. My smile faltered. Clearly, I had messed up. What did I do wrong? I wondered if I should retreat to the ladies room and check for pepper in my teeth one more time?

I stood there with my hand-outstretched waiting for one of them to shake it. Should I put my hand down? After what seemed like an eternity, one of them finally told me with the biggest eye roll I've ever seen, "Uhhhhh, we're not here for that thingy or whatever is going on here." EEEEK!!! Where is a sinkhole when you need one?

Has something like this ever happened to you? Do you have questions bombarding your mind about these same things when you try to step out of your comfort zone? Is it fear of this kind of scenario that has kept you from networking in the past? Well, there is good news. I'm here to save you from all those awkward and embarrassing moments that will make you feel like the only person in the room who doesn't know the secret to being successful at networking.

This book will provide you with the practical knowledge, and therefore the confidence, you need to step into any networking situation with the tools and insight to make it a productive method for advancing your business connections. I'll even share some of my networking war stories with you. I remember what it was like to be a beginner in the networking world and I didn't have anyone to ask. I had to learn everything the hard way but you don't have to learn networking the way I did. I will share with you the real secret to networking that is actually fun and gets results. It's most likely radically different than what you've previously been told or heard. I'll demystify networking and open your mind to the enormous potential of gaining business contacts through simple and effective techniques. By the time you finish this book, you'll understand how to make networking work for you. You will never fear being that lone clueless person standing with your hand out waiting to get laughed at.

There is a certain etiquette, or protocol, that is expected when it comes to business networking and few beginners have any idea what that entails and therefore they make a lot of errors that can sabotage their efforts. I did a lot of things wrong when I first started and my goal is to help you avoid making the same mistakes. It's okay if you don't know everything when you first get started. Nobody does. We all have to learn. What is important is having a willingness to admit that you need help and then listen to experts who can skillfully guide you on the right course.

Not knowing isn't shameful; it's continuing to not know that will get you into trouble. People will forgive you for being an unschooled newbie for a while but if you never attempt to become educated then you will most assuredly lose respect and potential business opportunities will vanish.

There is one gentleman that I know who I've seen jump from business venture to business venture but he never quite finds the success he desires. He is extremely pushy and doesn't understand that his approach to networking is driving people away from him as fast as they can run. His tactics scream 'desperation' and nobody even wants to greet him after their first encounter. They immediately walk the other direction when he appears because they know a simple hello will lead to being cornered by someone who monopolizes their time with an over the top sales pitch. They know this because time and again it has happened and they stand there wishing their phone would ring or that someone would rescue them from his relentless sales assault. You don't want to be like him. If you put in the time and effort to network, then make sure you develop the skill needed to make it a constructive method for building your business contacts and not something that works against you.

I embarked on the wonderful journey into entrepreneurship in 2007 when I started a home staging business. At that time, I didn't network at all. I relied solely on word of mouth referrals and that worked somewhat. Growth was extremely slow but at this time in my life I was okay with that, or at least that's what I told myself. I made lots of excuses as to why I couldn't network: I was too busy, it cost too much, I didn't know where to go, and I already knew plenty of people. The truth is, I was shy and didn't think that was the scene was for me. I couldn't picture myself strolling around some gathering or party and randomly introducing myself to strangers and starting conversations with them. Networking wasn't something that I could ever imagine myself doing, let alone being good at.

Then in 2010, I had an idea to create a website that talked about life from a woman's perspective. I called it Woman's InSite. At this same time, I was going through a divorce and many people thought I was foolish or crazy for taking this step because I lacked the business and computer skills most would think necessary to start any kind of business let alone an online one.

I knew I was capable of learning what I needed to when it came to the website, so I made it my priority and learned! I think my willingness to jump in and risk making some mistakes during the process is what gave me the courage to get the business off the ground and then keep moving forward when things got tough.

I spent about six months, and most of my money, getting the website up and running. While the webmaster was building the site, I worked on creating content for the launch. Once it was live, I had no idea how I was going to spread the word. I had this beautiful website but didn't understand how to let people know I was there. I planned to sell sponsorships to make money from the site so I needed to get traffic quickly if I was going to stay afloat. I hadn't thought ahead about needing some kind of budget for advertising when I was developing the site. Since I had no serious marketing money to speak of, people told me I should do some networking.

They made it sound so simple: just go to some events, meet some people and, like magic, they would flock to the business. But I was reluctant because I just knew it wasn't that easy. If it was, all their businesses would be swimming in money, but they weren't. I was also about as green as one could possibly be when it came to how to go about actually networking. I didn't have a lot of self-confidence to begin with and it all seemed very intimidating. I knew what "networking" was but I really had no idea how to approach strangers in a networking environment and then convert that to new business. However, even though I was shy, I realized I didn't have a lot of options, so I decided to give networking a try and see where it got me.

My first step was to throw a launch party for Woman's InSite so I could officially introduce my website to family and friends. About 60 people showed up which was a great turn out for my first try. I displayed the website on a large screen at the event and everybody thought it was wonderful. Food and drinks were served and all had a great time. But the next day it was business as usual for everyone and my inbox remained empty. I had all those people in a room for the party but no system in place to keep my website on their mind so there was little to no traffic. I certainly couldn't afford to host a party every month to create excitement and the one party I held hadn't produced any results anyway. These were all people that cared about me but they lived busy lives. They weren't all going to visit my website on a regular basis no matter how supportive they wanted to be. Besides, I needed way more than 60 people viewing my site consistently to make it a viable marketing tool for potential sponsors. People are bombarded with information these days and

I realized that I was forgotten about as fast as they drove away from that launch party. I knew that I was going to have to do more. I needed a way to reach new people, and a lot more of them, while at the same time keeping them interested! Networking seemed like a possible solution.

Initially, I joined a few small networking groups that met for lunch. I thought if I could just make friends with a few regulars it would make showing up a little easier – which it did. I quickly learned that seeing a few familiar faces settled my nerves and made talking with those I didn't know much less stressful. At times, I forced myself through uncomfortable situations to get out there and make connections. I knew if I wasn't willing to push my own boundaries I could never grow my business or myself.

Once I got the starting time wrong for a meeting and arrived late after everyone had already taken seats at a long table and the meeting had begun. I was mortified when I opened the door to the room and saw all eyes land on me as I walked around the long table trying to find a place to sit. It's a good thing that most luncheon events don't revolve around alcohol or I may have been tempted to order a glass of wine or a tequila shot to try and get past the awkwardness of the situation. That probably wouldn't have made any better impression on the attendees than my showing up late did.

At these small meetings, I proceeded to network like crazy to get the word out about my website. I talked to people I didn't know at every single event and looked for ways we might work together. I asked them for ideas on how they promoted their business to get ideas that might help me. I also asked everyone I knew about other networking events in the area and went to every single one I heard about. I tried them all! I needed website traffic and saw no other way to get the word out given my limited budget and experience. Being shy wasn't going to cut it. I had to find a way to cope with my insecurities and still get the job done. There were several techniques I used to get past my fear.

I discovered that if I arrived at events early that there weren't so many people to meet upon entering the room. That helped. It was easier for me to have people approach me as they came into the room rather than have all eyes on me expecting me to make the first move. I also made an effort to make friends with the hosts of events who usually made a point to introduce me to people so I didn't have to approach them cold. This helped me feel a little more like I belonged and was part of the group.

Standing up in front of a room full of people at networking events and talking about my business was great preparation for what I do today but at first it was very hard. We'll talk more about becoming a speaker later, but even at those first meetings I quickly realized the benefits that could be gained from being the one speaking at an event rather than just attending. The confidence boost networking gave me created the courage to tackle public speaking, which I had never done before. As I conquered my fear a little at a time, I spoke at numerous networking groups. I began each speech by telling my story of going from a housewife and volunteer, to entrepreneur. After those experiences proved successful, I developed a networking class and continued to improve on my speaking skills. Those that knew me, or heard my story, were inspired and motivated to step out in spite of their own fear.

I will be the first to say that speaking has opened many doors for me. While it was completely outside my personal comfort zone, it did get easier over time. I would have never imagined even a few years ago that an incredibly shy person like me would become a teacher or professional speaker. Now, I not only get paid to speak, I lead workshops and provide personal consulting on networking techniques, creating introductions, body language, self confidence, business and social media etiquette, and even how to become a speaker. It's amazing what you can do when failure isn't an option.

I don't intend to make it sound easy, it wasn't, but it wasn't as impossible as I assumed it to be either. Let me tell you about my first speaking opportunity. I did not go willingly! I was pretty much forced into it kicking and screaming. I had been attending this particular networking lunch group for about 18 months. They met once a month. Each month, we had to drop our card in a bowl that was used to randomly draw for the following month's speaker. Each time the host would draw a card, I would silently pray; Please, don't pick me! Don't pick me!

Of course, eventually, my card did get pulled out of that bowl and I was scheduled to be the next month's speaker. I was horrified and, of course, panicked! A friend calmly reminded me that I had a whole month to prepare and I only had to speak for ten minutes. I couldn't even imagine how I was going to stand in front of a room full of people and talk to the entire room for ten whole minutes. That seemed like eternity to me. I was wisely advised to share my story of how I went from being a woman with very limited business experience and computer skills to an entrepreneur who owned and managed a successful web-based business.

I determined that my first step was to write down what I wanted to say. I've always had a talent for putting words together so this part wasn't difficult. After that, I made some notes on notecards and practiced my speech several times in front of the mirror. By this time, I'd made some great friends in the networking world and invited them to come support me in my first attempt at public speaking. I knew that it would help to know there were friendly faces smiling back at me; people who would still care about me even if I messed things up. I'd come a long way since my first networking event but I was still extremely nervous about standing in front of a room and speaking for ten minutes.

When it came time for my speech, I felt like I wanted to run. As I looked out in the audience, I saw so many familiar faces of people that I knew had come just to hear me, there was no way I was going to let them down. Many friends had driven long distances to support me and hear me speak. I knew they'd be kind no matter how it turned out and I realized it really didn't matter if it wasn't perfect.

The speech itself was all kind of a blur to me. I didn't remember exactly what I'd said when I finished but I was tremendously relieved I'd gotten through it without making an absolute fool of myself. Then, as people approached me afterward, I was shocked at how many friends and even complete strangers congratulated me and told me how I had inspired and motivated them. I had no idea that what I said would have that kind of effect on people. It was a real eye-opener for me.

I had asked a friend to record the event so I could critique myself afterward. Later, when I watched the video, I was surprised at how poised I seemed because on the inside, I was a bundle of nerves. After I had time to reflect, I felt pretty good about the experience and was amazed at the number of people that asked me to come and speak at their networking groups. That first attempt opened so many doors and revealed how powerful speaking could be for me. Now, I'm so glad I managed to set aside my fears for just a few minutes and give it a try.

After several years of networking, meeting all kinds of people, and figuring out how to turn connections into business opportunities by trial and error, I developed specific networking principles that work based on real world experience. I quickly recognized there was a market for this information and enthusiastically taught others what I'd learned. Just like me, these people were looking for answers on how networking really works and how to make it work for them. Over the years, I have seen many people approach networking with immaturity or, even worse, old school tactics and end up making all kinds of mistakes that can easily be avoided. Seasoned networkers observe each other, as well as those new to networking, and make judgments. If those first impressions are negative they can be very difficult to overcome, but not impossible. I know that feeling of being a bumbling newbie as I was just that not long ago. After some success in teaching my networking class to different groups, in 2014 I established the Kathryn C. Wheat School of Real Estate to teach networking skills to Realtors.

This was a huge step. Don't forget how anxious I confessed to being at the beginning! When I spoke the first time I was so nervous that after visiting the restroom several times, my friend ordered a glass of wine for me in the hopes it would settle me down enough to stay out of the bathroom. I drank half of it before I got up to speak. Thankfully, I no longer need that kind of liquid courage, or anything else, to calm my nerves, which is a good thing, or I might have developed a reputation for being a lush!

What I learned I did not come by easily and I desperately wished someone had handed me a book that contains exactly what I'm going to share with you and teach you. The networking concepts I teach include:

- How to prepare yourself to network.

- How to brand yourself to lend credibility to your online presence.

- How to make a good first impression.

- How to overcome fear and confidently meet new people.

- How to greet business people appropriately.

- How to engage properly in conversation with other networkers.

- How to create a great introduction.

- How and where to network.
- How to understand and prioritize the different kinds of organized networking groups.
- How to stand out in a good way.
- How to understand the buzzwords you may hear.
- How to employ effective conversations tips.
- How to prevent one person from dominating your time at an event.
- How body language can enhance your networking efforts.
- How to stay in touch with your new connections.
- How to deal with that huge stack of business cards that you acquire from attending networking events.
- How to decipher and prioritize which contacts to spend your time meeting with, who to add to your email list, and who not to waste your time on.

If you implement the tools and techniques within this book, you will not only be able to increase your network and grow your business, you will also have more confidence when it comes to making new connections and meeting the movers and shakers in your field.

The basis of Networking: Naked & Unafraid isn't about joining a nudist colony! It is about how to discover your true and authentic self and then present that to the people you want to do business with. People respond to those who are genuine and that is the first and most important lesson you will learn in this book. Networking isn't about convincing people you are someone you aren't just so they will buy whatever you are selling. It is about letting them get to know the real you. And don't worry; you can actually keep your clothes on!

Strip Down

"Networking is simply starting a conversation with no destination in mind."

~ Kathryn Crawford Wheat

1

A Conversation with
no Destination

According to Webster's Dictionary, networking is defined as: the exchange of information or services among individuals, groups, or institutions, specifically the cultivation of productive relationships for employment or business.

I don't know about you; but that definition sounds about as exciting as watching grass grow. Yawn! Many times in my workshops I ask people their definition of networking. I get many varied responses but the common thread is that it's the act of meeting people that you can do business with. While all of the above is certainly true, I have narrowed it down to one definition and fundamental principal, which, if embraced, will give you a huge advantage among all of the other networkers out there. Networking is simply the act of starting a conversation with no destination in mind.

Here's the important part: don't start a conversation with your only goal being to make a sale. I understand this may seem counterintuitive but consider this, if all you are thinking about is selling something to the person in front of you then it will be displayed in your expressions and through your body language no matter how much you think you are a smooth operator. Don't walk into a room and start sizing people up looking for prospects. They will sense that you want something from them and will run from you just like they would a used car salesman. Think about this; how do you feel when someone approaches you and immediately launches a sales pitch? You probably want to get away from them as fast as possible. So, why do that to someone else?

The motive for attending a networking event is not to sell. I'm sure this may go against everything you've been told. In fact, you probably think its crazy, but selling shouldn't be your primary goal. Remember, you are out there networking to start conversations with no destination in mind. You shouldn't go out meeting people with the sole purpose of looking for clients or closing a deal. Understand that you will meet the right people eventually and it's not in your best interest to force connections when they aren't there. It just leads to unhappy results for both parties. Your purpose is to make friends and connections within the business community so that other people will talk about you. It's much better for someone else to go around saying great things about you than for you to walk around tooting your own horn and bragging about how great you are at what you do. Let others do that for you, and they will if you let them.

Many people are familiar with the Oprah effect. That is the idea that if your book, gadget, song and dance show or whatever gets listed as one of Oprah's favorite things, your business experiences a meteoric rise in sales and you hit the big time. Having her endorsement is far better than any advertising or horn tooting you can possibly do for yourself! Unfortunately we don't all personally know Oprah, but we do know influential people that can help us grow our connections and businesses simply by them telling others great things about us. That is why you network!

Building a valuable network is important but it's vital to respect the people in your network. As soon as someone starts feeling used, they are likely to stop taking your calls, answering your emails or telling their friends about you. I like to be supportive of my friends just because I like them even if I'm not in the market for what they're selling. If they don't push me to buy their product or services, I'm much more likely to recommend them to my friends who are in the market for what they sell. I only make referrals for people I'm proud to be associated with. I'm sure you feel the same way. Every referral I make is a direct reflection on me. When people get too pushy, they end up on top of the "do not answer or refer list".

I think we all know people who are addicted to "great new opportunities" and constantly hop from one business to the next searching for financial freedom. You may not hear from them for months but as soon as they join a new venture, you can bet your name is on their list of who to call and tell about this "fantastic business opportunity" that you just have to get in on. We all know someone like this and every time the phone rings and their number pops up, we hesitate, because we know it's probably a pitch – and we just don't want to hear it.

However, people who have a strong, vibrant network don't have to be pushy. Have you ever met a top realtor or financial advisor or other industry leader? The first thing you notice is that they have no interest in selling you anything. They are interesting people because they are interested in you. They want to know what your business is about, what your hopes and dreams are, what makes you tick. If you run across one of these people, hang out within earshot and listen. Listen to how they introduce themselves, how they engage in conversations, what questions they ask. You will find that they actually do very little talking and a great deal of listening. Yet after people meet them, they tell others how wonderful they are. They don't need to push anything and by not pushing, they become leaders in their fields.

So remember, never try to "sell" someone at a networking event. Nothing will get people running from you faster than being pushy and expecting them to whip out their credit card and buy your product or service on the spot. Do you like it when someone is trying to "sell" you? Of course not! Remember the golden rule? "Do unto others as you would have them do unto you." Call it Karma or whatever you want, just respect other people by not forcing your products and services on them. Whatever you put out there will come back to you. You reap what you sow!

You can't expect change to happen if you're not willing to make changes. Continuing to do things that aren't productive will just waste your time and most likely hurt your reputation. Make a commitment now to be proactive and make some key changes that will minimize your wasted effort and increase your productivity when it comes to networking, and then make an effort to get to know people first. Try not to immediately start thinking of how you can sell something as soon as you meet someone. They can tell when they are being sized up. Instead, take time to let a relationship develop and see where it takes you. Be open to different possibilities for new relationships other than making the immediate sale. Discover who they know. Even if you have to take tiny little steps, just stay focused and keep improving.

You can think of networking like speed dating. When you meet someone for the first time, you wouldn't start your first conversation with the assumption that you are going to have a relationship with that person. It's just the initial meeting. You don't even know whether or not you will like that person or if they're going to like you. It's way too soon to start picking out names for your children. It's the same way with networking. You will start many conversations and then go on to continue the dialogue with the few that you connect with.

Just start the conversation! Then you can decipher who you want to continue getting to know better.

You won't connect with everyone and that's perfectly fine so don't set expectations that you will. Your market isn't everyone; it is just those select few individuals with whom you have a connection. Have an open mind; a simple hello can lead to a million possibilities. With practice, you'll learn to quickly evaluate and determine who you want to develop a closer business relationship with, and who isn't a good fit.

When I first started my website, (WomansInSite.com), I didn't understand this basic principle. I did business with a few people that I knew were a bad fit for my website and for me. I regretted it pretty quickly.

In the beginning, I was begging for contributing writers and agreed to take an article from an interior designer that I suspected would need a lot of guidance, but I was desperate for content and agreed to take his post. I should have trusted my instincts when he submitted the photo that was to appear next to his post. It was a snapshot of him with his cat snuggled up to his face, not very professional at all. When he finally submitted his article, there were no punctuation marks at all! I spent more time trying to figure out and edit what he'd written than I would have spent researching and writing the post myself. Clearly, he was a better designer than he was a writer. Then to make matters worse, he was extremely insulted that I'd edited his article so much! Desperation generally results in bad decisions.

Other times, I've met people and immediately knew the connection was going to be a great fit. Through networking I found the bookkeeper that I use for my business and she is the sweetest, most trustworthy person you'll ever meet. I knew right away that we'd click! Right after our initial meeting, I asked her to meet the next week so we could talk and I hired her on the spot. She's been doing my books ever since. Before I met her, I met about ten other bookkeepers and just didn't get that warm fuzzy feeling about them. Having patience is necessary. Wait for the right fit. It's out there.

"You can't become
who you need to be
by remaining
who you are."

~ Kathryn Crawford Wheat

2

Growth Requires Change

I will never forget my very first large networking event. It was at a national women's conference with about 80 other women and a few brave men. I had no idea what to expect. I just thought I'd jump in and see what happened. My former business partner and I took our seats at a table and listened to announcements outlining how the day would unfold. As we listened to the speaker, it soon became alarmingly clear to us that we would be expected to stand up in front of the room and give our name and a few seconds of introduction about our business. As this unfolded, I noticed that many people had memorized catchy phrases or rhymes that had the audience clapping for them as they finished speaking. This is what I now understand to be the classic "elevator pitch". We nervously whispered back and forth about who would be the one to stand up and speak. We were totally unprepared, frightened and intimidated at the thought of speaking in front of a room full of people. She somehow convinced me that I was the obvious choice and I promised that I would try my best not to blow it. I was just as nervous as she was but her encouragement pushed me forward. Besides, she looked like she was almost completely paralyzed with fear. Then we realized that we were both actually expected to stand up and speak! That's when her nerves got the best of her. As we watched each person stand up and speak, she actually broke out in hives that covered her neck and chest at the thought of going through with this activity. I wasn't sure if her legs would still work when she tried to stand up.

It's funny to look back at this moment because from my perspective today, this doesn't seem like a big deal at all. I've managed to successfully stand up in front of thousands of people countless times and have never had anyone make fun or point fingers at me. I've learned that business networkers are mostly kind individuals who empathize with those who are nervous. They understand that for some people, speaking in front of a room full of people can be nerve wracking, especially when you are new to the networking scene.

I know now that with each occurrence, standing up in front of a crowded room gets easier but during that first conference we were in complete panic mode. Eventually it came around the room and it was our turn to stand up and speak. My business partner did just fine and really, no one but me knew how nervous she was. I also managed to pull it off without sounding like a blubbering idiot. It was a great learning experience for both of us. We were forced to learn on the fly and we survived! Remember that staying in your comfort zone will prevent progress and sometimes being forced to take that next step is a good thing.

I noticed that many people at the women's conference had these catchy little sound bite-type phrases that they recited when they stood up to introduce themselves. I thought I'd better get something like this together. I wanted to sound like I knew what I was doing when I stood up to give my "elevator pitch".

There are many well-intentioned coaches and consultants out there teaching networkers how to develop a "pitch" that they stress must be delivered immediately upon meeting someone. Here's what I think about that now: don't waste your money! Some networkers actually spend hours writing a pitch, memorizing it, rehearsing it, timing it and trying to get it perfect.

The problem with "pitches" is that they're fake. The sound fake; they feel fake. It's not how you would normally approach someone and it never comes off smooth and authentic no matter how much you practice. It's like a bad pick up line. They're lame and do nothing to get people interested in what you do. In fact, they just creep people out and make them want to turn around and walk away. When "pitches" are made, people feel awkward and it makes everyone involved feel uncomfortable. People suddenly feel pressured to respond. It's like someone asking you to marry them on the big screen at a sporting event! What do you say? Nobody likes to be on the receiving end of a "pitch". I certainly don't and I'm sure you don't either.

A big problem with new networkers is that they think they have to do things like everybody else when they don't realize that many of those people aren't making good impressions themselves. It's a never-ending cycle of people doing what they see everyone else do assuming it must be appropriate. They don't understand that to stand out from the pack, all they have to do is be genuine and authentic.

Because I thought I had to be like everybody else, I actually paid a coach a whole lot of money to help me develop the perfect "elevator pitch". I filled out a questionnaire and sent it to him. He helped me edit it to about 3 or 4 sentences that described what I did, who I was looking for, and how I could help them. Then he added in a couple of words that rhymed and told me it was ready to go. I memorized it, practiced it, and perfected it in front of the mirror. I felt certain I was ready to give it a go so at my next lunch meeting I stood up, recited my lines perfectly and waited for the accolades! I knew I had nailed it! But to my astonishment, no applause followed and even worse, I had a room full of people looking back at me with perplexity and sympathy. Not being one to give up easily, I gave it a shot several more times.

Needless to say, I didn't get the results I hoped for. In fact, it fell completely flat every time! I wanted to give up and go home never to return to the networking scene. I felt like a failure at "pitching". I felt like it just wasn't me and I didn't think I could do it. I was right! I'm no good at "pitching", but on the other hand, I'm really good at being me just as you are really good at being you!

Now don't misunderstand me here, you do need to be able to talk about your business and what you do in a concise, professional manner. We'll go more in depth on what to say and how to say it later, but for now, just understand that being the most authentic version of you is the very first step.

Let's talk a little bit about the "C" word. I'm talking about competition. Many networkers complain that there are too many people from their same industry or profession in the networking world. They fear the competition is too tough and therefore never give it a try. At least this is one of the concerns I hear when I teach my workshops and speak on networking. I'd like you to consider changing your view of competition. My view of competition is a little different than most other people's view. I believe that success is infinite. There isn't a limited supply. There is plenty to go around! In fact, when you see your competitors achieving success, let that motivate you. They are proof that what you are trying to achieve can be done. Don't worry about what your competition is doing or how successful they appear to be. You have no way of knowing how hard they've had to work or what they've been through to get where they are now. But you do know that it is possible.

I encourage you to make friends with other people in your industry or profession. This is a great way to develop strategic partnerships and learn from each other, so play nice. If you are genuinely kind to your competitors, good things will come to you. It creates good will. Occasionally you will meet people that just seem to have success fall from the universe right into their lap. Jealousy can take over and get the best of us all but try to remember not to let that get in the way of your own success and growth. Instead, stay focused on what you are doing to further your own career. Everyone has different strengths and perspectives that they bring to the table. When you connect with your competitors, you can help each other grow if you have confidence in yourself. Instead of being competitive with each other, think about being cooperative. Work together to make a bigger impact in your industry.

In my experience, I've seen many people struggle with the idea of healthy competition. Understand that healthy competition will make you stronger, faster, better. It's a good thing! We don't have to try to stay away from one another or undermine those in the same profession, as it will not help us. If you happen to already be super successful in your field, help those who are just learning. Take the time to offer some free advice. There were probably people who mentored you as well. This can be a way to give back.

I recommend that you stay away from drama or it will ultimately cause you to lose what you've been working so hard to achieve. The networking world can be very small and word will get around quickly if you are hateful toward others. There is room for each of us to prosper, so be respectful and kind to others along the way.

When it's possible, lend a hand to help other people. They will appreciate your efforts and won't forget how you helped them. I make it a point to include time on my calendar for mentoring. I love spending time with people who are where I was just a few years ago.

Many generous business people helped me along the way and I feel it is an honor to be able to give back in kind.

Think about it like this: You are your only competition. Believe in yourself and what you have to offer. Know that you are here to do business with people that relate to you. Understand that nobody is like you and nobody will ever have the same approach that you do. You will find the people that you are meant to do business with. Don't spend a single second worrying about who other people are reaching. Those people aren't meant for you.

Having said that, there will be times when you really mess things up. You will blow it, embarrass yourself (or others), or just drop the ball. It happens to us all. When you mess up, don't let it get you down. We all make mistakes. Own up to it and apologize. Then correct the problem and keep moving forward. Don't dwell on it or engage in self-sabotage. Failure is just a stepping-stone to success.

Think positive! Strive to go out each day with the intention of improving on what you did the day before. No need to waste time and energy worrying about what others are doing or how you may have failed. Instead, spend your time and energy looking for ways you can develop into the successful business person you aspire to be.

GET NAKED & UNAFRAID

"Because true belonging only happens when we present our authentic, imperfect selves to the world, our sense of belonging can never be greater than our level of self-acceptance."

~ Brene Brown

3

Now, for some Great News!

Because true belonging only happens when we present our authentic, imperfect selves to the world, our sense of belonging can never be greater than our level of self-acceptance. ~ Brene Brown

I believe that networking is the most effective and least expensive marketing method that you can use to develop your business and build your personal brand. If you have already tried networking and haven't found it to be effective, you might need to consider changing your approach. Networking the right way doesn't have to be complicated. I'm here to help you prepare and get started. If you follow my step-by-step approach that I've developed from years of experience, you will see how a few basic but core principles will simplify your efforts and get you started making tons of legitimate business connections. Those connections will accelerate your ability to grow your business in a short amount of time.

People want to know who you are before they will care what you do. There's no need to be phony and put on a false face. So many people think they have to put on a show and recite their lines like actors in a movie. The pressure to get it right can cripple you just like a bad case of stage freight. When this happens, it totally defeats the purpose of networking because you aren't showing up as you. You are just playing a part, a role. Remove your cloak and be yourself. There's nothing you have to hide.

The problem with working on and memorizing that "perfect pitch" is you are not being true to yourself. Understand that all you need to do is be honest and transparent, in effect, naked. You want people to see through the façade and past the window dressing and see who you are when everything's stripped away. If you are naked, meaning realistic and authentic, you don't have to be afraid that they might find you out at some point! Remove those layers of "salesperson" training and get back to being a real, honest genuine human being. Strip down to the real you and get out there and network!

You must cast aside every bit of who you think you are supposed to be. Forget all you've been told about how to "pitch" or "sell". Peel off every layer of how you think you are supposed to dress and act, and what you are supposed to say. Get down to who you truly are at the core. That's the person that needs to show up. That's the person that people want to know. Not some fake character with a scripted "sales pitch". People will appreciate you for being your genuine self and that's what will attract them to you. So don't be afraid to be yourself. Don't think you have to act exactly like your competitors act. Find your own unique approach. You are good enough completely naked!

There is a man who owns a very successful furniture store in the Houston, TX area that started his business with $5,000 and a truck. His name is Jim McInvale and he is the owner and founder of Gallery Furniture. Initially his business did fairly well but back in the 80's when the oil market took a downturn, his business experienced a serious decline. He decided to spend his last $10,000 on airtime for TV commercials. He had a script written for him but was unhappy with the way it sounded and decided to just ad lib. He had to talk very fast in order to say everything he wanted to say since he had limited time on the commercial. Then at the end he pulled money out of his pocket, jumped up and yelled, "Gallery Furniture saves you money!" It was goofy and nerdy and everybody thought it was funny. But it worked. He was simply being himself and it endeared others to him. That phrase became what he's known for and Gallery Furniture has grown into a multimillion-dollar business consisting of several stores.

Let's all try and be our authentic messy selves. Accept that we occasionally have hurdles that cause us to stumble. Go ahead, laugh and even cry but own it. Only then we can attract the people who fit with who we are. It's not always easy, but we can find great joy in discovering who we are and who we are meant to connect with.

I urge you, figure out who you are and see where that takes you. When you are simply spending time with your friends, how do you act? Think about what you like to do in your recreational time. What kinds of things are priorities in your life? If you were talking to a good friend about your business, what would you say? Why do you like the business you are in? What's your favorite part? What's the bad part? Where do you plan to go with it? How do you approach your business in a way that may be different than someone else in a similar business? Start thinking about all of these things. Write them down. Add to the list as you think of more things. The answers to these questions will allow you to be able to define what makes you unique. Embrace all the things that you have written down, the good part and the part that may need a little improvement. We are all a work in progress.

When you do this, you'll realize there's no effort or fear involved in being you. It comes naturally. I know from experience that if you will let go of that networker you thought you had to be, you will be more relaxed and will get a more honest and desirable response from

45

people you meet. The idea of being yourself is a huge relief if you've been working diligently at being somebody else. It's like a weight being lifted off your shoulders. Once you get down to your core, to that person you really are and want to be, to the naked part of yourself that is completely authentic, it makes showing up so much easier. In fact, I think you'll find that you actually want to show up because there is no longer any pressure. When you understand that you don't have to try to be something you are not, the fear will fade away and you will realize that you have absolutely nothing to lose.

When I was a child I hated having curly hair. Nobody else in my family had curls so it seemed like the fact that I had a head full of them created a lot of unwanted attention from my perspective as a child. People would ask my mother where my curls came from and she would just say she didn't know. Of course there were the inevitable winks and jokes like, "What did the mailman look like?" which I didn't quite understand but it always made people laugh. For the record, I happen to look very much like my father. The point is that all of this attention caused me to hate having curly hair. I used to actually cry and say, "No curls, is it?" asking for my mother to confirm what I so desperately desired. But the fact remained that I do have curly hair.

When I grew up, I learned how to straighten my hair and wore it that way for a number of years. Now, I embrace my head full of curls because it is an authentic part of who I am. It's actually become part of my personal brand. I'm recognized and known for my curls. In fact, when I occasionally straighten my hair, people that know me don't recognize me because I look so different. They actually walk right past me and don't realize it's me until I speak to them. So if there is something about you that stands out, use it to your advantage and make it part of your personal brand. An illustrator/ cartoonist who is a very good friend of mine, David Bamberg, even did a caricature of me that emphasizes my curls. I love it!

"A brand is no longer what we tell the customer it is — it is what customers tell each other it is."

~ Scott Cook

4

Time to get Branded

Now that you know that it is okay to be you, you must decide who you are and what name you want to go by. How do you want to present yourself and be known in the business community? These are the questions that you must answer before you start meeting people. If you aren't sure who you are, how can you possibly tell others? This is known as branding.

The word branding can be very confusing because so many people use it to mean different things. Your brand is who and what you stand for as a company and as a person. To simplify it, it is your reputation. That is why I tell people that they need to brand their personal name. Don't get this confused with the business name. You will still work under your business name but remember people do business with people. They will identify with you as an individual first and you are your brand. You are the name and face that people will associate with your business or product.

For instance, we all know of Steve Jobs and Sir Richard Branson. We also know that Apple is where Steve Jobs made a huge contribution to the way we use mobile devices and that Sir Richard Branson is known for creating over 400 companies in the Virgin Group but is mostly known for Virgin Airways and Virgin Mobile. If someone says the name Steve Jobs to you, what do you think about? First of all you are going to picture Steve Jobs, not the Apple Corporation, and then you are going to think about the apple logo, iPhone or a MAC computer. If someone mentions Sir Richard Branson, what do you think about? You picture the man and then you think about his empire, Virgin Group.

Having name/face recognition is very valuable when marketing your business whether you are a small entrepreneur or creator of a huge corporation. The point is that we know these people as individuals and have emotions tied to the person, not necessarily the corporation. In your mind, the person is the company.

Remember, I said that people want to know who you are before they want to know what you do.

Tom Peters, world-renowned brand guru and bestselling author of the book "In Search of Excellence" stated, Big companies understand the importance of brands. Today, in the age of the individual, you have to be your own brand. It's time for me - and you - to take a lesson from the big brands, a lesson that's true for anyone who's interested in what it takes to stand out and prosper in the world of work.

In this age of the new media, meaning Internet, we all have access to the masses. What you do with that access is up to you. Your credibility, recognition and circle of influence within your business community are indispensable for your personal brand as well as your company's corporate brand. A company who recognizes the importance of hiring individuals with strong personal brands is a company that will undoubtedly have an edge when it comes to building a team of recognized authorities within a particular industry that bring new audiences and tribes to the boardroom with them. When you join a corporation and bring your tribe into the fold, you become a very valuable asset to that corporation. A company who is privileged enough to employ people with strong personal brands has a major advantage over its competitors.

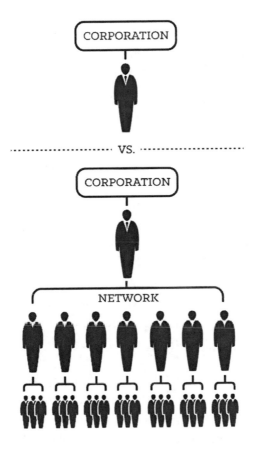

In the past, it was all about the company. A great marketing campaign would tell you everything about what a company provided and what vital element you were missing if you didn't partake in the product or service they had to offer. But there has been a marketing shift that allows us to market through networking and social media and this has changed everything.

People want to know who is talking. We want to see proof that there is a qualified person behind the information we are being given. People want to have face-to-face conversations with a valued and knowledgeable representative of the company and not just a marketing expert who may not really understand everything behind the fancy ad campaign. A marketer may not know how to properly engage in conversations about your company, which can call into question the credibility of the information being presented. A valued person within the company understands the information and is a much better choice to handle the task of representing the company's products or services.

Without this face-to-face interaction, we are less likely to trust what we are being told via nameless, faceless advertising and marketing. Networking provides excellent opportunities for us to go out and get that face-to-face interaction and form real connections with our customers as well as others who may become advocates for our company. There is power in networking. Not because you are selling directly to those you meet, but because you will form valuable business connections with people who will be inspired and motivated to market for you. You will form a community of people who are mutually excited about sharing what each of you does with their individual communities.

This is why you should brand your personal name. Let me explain. Do you own your name as a dot com? I want to be very clear here as I run across some confusion in my classes when I talk about this. I'm not talking about setting up an email like KathrynWheat@ AOL.com or KathrynWheat@gmail.com. I'm talking about using your personal name as the actual dot com or (Universal Resource Locator) URL. Then you can have your name as your email address and it will be very easy for people to remember. If you make it easy for people to find you, they're much more likely to do business with you. For instance, I have the URL KathrynWheat.com and I use the email address Kathryn@KathrynWheat.com. I don't recommend using some of the other domain extensions that are out there such as dot net, dot realtor, or dot biz as your domain. Dot com is still the most common and widely recognized. Using your personal name alleviates confusion and you can directly link that personal site to your business site as well. So it doesn't matter if they look up your business or you personally, they can still find you very easily.

It's very important to register your name and own it as a dot com. You can go to any domain registrar and search to see if your name is available to register. GoDaddy is the most common one but I like Wilsher Media Group, which is an affiliate of GoDaddy. If your name is available then get it registered right away. If you have a very common name like Bob Smith then you can consider using your middle initial or your middle name, such as, BobCSmith.com or BobCarlSmith. com. If those are still taken then you can try TheBobSmith.com. The point is to use your personal name in some form or fashion. Once you settle on what name you will use, then be very consistent and "BRAND" it by using it everywhere and on everything.

The reason you need to do this is so you can start building a name for yourself via the Internet. When someone meets you, and wants to know more about you, guess what they do? They will put your name into a search engine to see what they can find out about you on the Internet. This happens more often than you realize and it's vitally important for you to have control over what people see. Even if there are many people on the Internet with your same name, if you've successfully branded you, then they will be able to differentiate which stories are about you and what stories are about someone else. This is why using current pictures in your Internet branding is very important, especially if you have a common name. When somebody who is searching for information about you sees a link with your picture, they will know that they have the right Bob Smith.

There are several things that can happen if you don't take this important step. If someone searches your name and they don't find anything at all, it looks like you are not established and you haven't done anything memorable. You look like an amateur or a newbie with no experience. People want to do business with people that have an established reputation. It's kind of like not having a credit score. You can't get anywhere with a non-existent credit score. You, as a person, shouldn't be non-existent online either. If you resist this step, you will soon be forgotten as one of those who refused to embrace the new media. People are going to search for you, that is a given; it's up to you to provide them with something positive and memorable to see.

Let's say that you have the same name as someone who has a lot of unfavorable press. Maybe it is a "has been" celebrity or disgraced politician who just happens to share your name. Just like a bad credit score, it can hamper your ability to gain respect. If this is all people see, and you haven't established a positive online presence, it leaves people guessing. The ramifications of not having control over your online presence can stifle your ability to establish yourself in business. You must be proactive in establishing your own Internet identity to combat any confusion there may be about who you are. Don't let people searching for you get confused with that person online that has a train wreck of a reputation.

It's up to you to take charge of what is being seen when your name is put into a search engine. Having your name as a dot com, and putting something online that you are in control of, is a big step in ensuring that when people search for you online it produces a positive result. Trust me, if someone's considering starting any kind of business relationship with you they will check you out. If you haven't registered your own personal name as a dot com I strongly urge you to stop what you are doing right now and take this step. It's surprisingly inexpensive and easy to do so there are NO excuses.

You can either lead the conversation or you can ignore it. You can't do anything about what other people put on the Internet but you can certainly make sure that you provide positive impressions of the real you and what you have to offer. So develop your own online presence under your personal name. It's okay if there is someone else online with your same name. Once you start branding yourself, your information will begin showing up in searches, which will increase the chances of prospective customers or clients finding you and being impressed.

There is more than one Kathryn Wheat out there, but if you Google my name, you will see a whole bunch of information that is about me along with my picture.

Here is a screen shot of what came up when I put my name in a Google search at the time I wrote this book:

In my networking classes, I often get asked whether women should use their maiden name or married name. Women have some decisions to make when it comes to branding their name. Whether you are married or single, just register the name that you have now. If you become married, divorced, or even re-married, you can register your new name and forward it to the name that you already have branded. It's very simple. I originally branded my name using my middle initial, KathrynCWheat.com, because my name was already taken. But just recently, my name became available so I have pointed everything I had previously branded to the simpler version, KathrynWheat.com. This is where I have my website with all the information anyone needs to find out more about what I do and how to book me.

I even registered several common misspellings of my name such as Katherine Wheat and Catherine Wheat because my name has many ways that it is commonly spelled. I have all those domain names forwarded to the correct place, KathrynWheat.com where I have established my online presence. As a result, when someone searches for my name, or any of the other versions of my name, I have a very positive presence that I have built on the Internet.

My good friend, Ronald Earl Wilsher of Branding for Humans™ and Wilsher Media Group is great at helping people navigate this necessary step. He is a Professional Branding Consultant and has helped me tremendously with building my own brand. You can find out more about him at RonaldWilsher.com. Don't put off getting your own name as a domain as it is a vital early step to really get started branding yourself!

Once you decide what name you want to brand, doing things like setting up social media accounts will help your rankings on search engines by getting more versions of the name you are using out there. We'll talk more about social media and how to utilize it later, but for now, just remember that the more visibility and links you have on the Internet, the higher your name will be seen in a search. If you have a website with your name as the dot com, that will come up first more often than not. I will caution you to have some patience with your Internet ranking once you start up a website and put some content out there. New rankings don't happen overnight and it may take a while for the various search engines to catch up, but it will happen. Consistency is the key!

Now if these are things you haven't even thought of and your eyes are glazing over at the thought of managing a full-blown website, don't panic. You don't have to do that. Think about setting up a simple landing page using your name, (example: RonaldWilsher. com) as the domain name. The domain name is what you type into whatever browser you use such as Safari, Internet Explorer, Google Chrome or Firefox to go to a particular website. For instance, if you wanted to look at Disney's website you would type Disney.com into the browser of your choice.

As you can see below, this landing page is a very simple, one page website that just has a name, photo, business logo and all the social media sites that Ronald is on right there on one page. This makes it easy for people to find all the places they can connect with him. There are links for his business websites and social media accounts on one page, which means if they want to click on the LinkedIn button, it will take them to his LinkedIn page. If they click on the company logo, it'll take them to his website. It's like one-stop shopping for all you need to know about Ronald Wilsher. You can create a similar page for yourself that has your social media and business information.

If you have a landing page, when people search for your name on the Internet, they will see your page come up in the search and your online presence will give you a great deal of credibility. Ronald Wilsher builds landing pages for his clients. His company makes changes as needed to keep it current so if you change jobs or want to add a link to your favorite charity then it can easily be edited. If building a page yourself is a little intimidating, you can contact him at RonaldWilsher.com. Here is what his landing page looks like:

Having your name and a website will also give you more power with search engines such as Google as well as help people find out about everything that you do. Most people are involved in more than one project and this is a great way to present all those ideas or companies in one easy to find place.

When I first launched my website, I didn't grasp the importance of branding my name as well. I just wanted to get the name of my website out there and known. I didn't have photos of me or even have my name anywhere on my site until after doing some networking, I finally understood that people connect with me personally first. It's after that connection is made that they want to know more about what I do.

Here's an amusing example that I found to illustrate what branding can do for you as opposed to what advertising, marketing and public relations can do for you. While they do all work together somewhat, it is important to know the differences in approach with each one and understand why the idea of branding is by far the strongest.

Marketing: Boy says to Girl, "I'm a great lover."

Public Relations: PR firm says to Girl, "Trust me, he's a great lover."

Advertising: Boy says to Girl, "I'm a great lover. I'm a great lover. I'm a great lover."

Branding: Girl says to Boy, "I hear you are a great lover?"

"Your business card
is a vital part of your
networking tool kit,
as it provides an
early snapshot of you
as an individual."

~ *Jon Visaisouk*

5

Business
Card

Let's talk about your business card for just a minute. Yes, you absolutely need to have one. No exceptions. It's how people will remember you and where they will look to find your contact information. If you don't hand out a card, you are forgotten as soon as you walk away. Even if you are involved in several business ventures, you only need one card. I've seen some business people carry around cards from each business they are in. Don't do this! Do you think Sir Richard Branson carries around business cards for each of the 400 companies that he owns? He'd need a suitcase! You only need one card that provides the basic information that someone would need who wants to get in touch with you. This means your logo, phone number, email address, website address and photo on a simple card. Don't create confusion by handing out several cards. You are wasting money having all those cards printed. Just get one simple but impressive card!

People will make quick judgments about you based on what your business card looks like. I know it may seem a little unrealistic, but that is how it is. Your business card has a lot to do with the kind of first impression business people will have about you. Think about it like this: if someone else wants to make a referral for you and hands out your card to a potential prospect for your business, what would your card say about you? You would want to make sure it's classy and that it sends a message of stability and professionalism. It's worth it to spend a little extra money on heavy paper. My card is printed on 16 pt. paper. It's nice and heavy. Please don't hand out a flimsy card that feels like copy paper! The difference in cost between 10 pt. and 16 pt. paper is miniscule but the difference in impact is huge. It's worth the little bit extra to make a professional impression. You'll be glad you did.

One interesting thing to note here; I win a lot of door prizes. My card gets pulled out so much that it's become a common joke that Kathryn Wheat has won again! The reason this happens is that the heavy paper stands out even in a fishbowl full of business cards. It has a nicer feel. If it stands out in a fishbowl, consider how well it will stand out when your potential client is holding it. Winning door prizes is a great perk, but the better reason for having that nice feeling card is to make a great first impression!

Some may think this goes without saying but unfortunately I've seen otherwise: make sure there are no typos on your card and the information is correct and up to date. Do not just mark out old information and handwrite in the current information. Spend the money and print new cards! When networking, you will meet people from all age groups and demographics. This includes the demographic of the over 40 crowd. As a member of that particular sector of business people, I can get away with poking fun at us. Please help us stay in denial about our increasing need for reading glasses. We would greatly appreciate it if you would use a font on your card that we can actually read.

Many times networking events are held in places where the lighting is dim making it even more challenging to read small print. Some cards have fonts so small, or scripts so fancy, that I have to get a magnifying glass to see what is written! Remember that simple is better and more information on your card isn't necessarily better if it can't be read. Even those with perfect vision will appreciate being able to glance at your card and easily read your name and number.

Another practical reason for using a larger font is that some people like to use a scanner or card reader to capture that information for their email list. It's almost impossible for those readers to pick up small fonts. Bigger is definitely better!

Your brand is your name and your face is your logo as far as networking is concerned. Yes, you may also have a company logo but you are who people identify with when it comes to business recognition. For this reason, it is extremely important to put a photo on your card. According to Wikipedia, approximately 60% - 65% of the population thinks in pictures as opposed to words. When you say a person's name, do you visualize the letters that make up their name or do you picture their face? If someone says the words "red corvette", do you picture the car or the words? Most of us identify with the picture. Having your picture on your card will help people remember you distinctly.

However, make sure the photo actually looks like you! I can't tell you how many times a person has handed a card to me and the photo on it looks nothing at all like the person standing in front of me. I feel embarrassed for them. Even if you love that old picture from college it may be time for a more current, business headshot. Please be careful about overly done hair and makeup. It's not appropriate for business headshots.

I like photo-shopped photos as much as the next person but be careful about overusing this miraculous tool. You must resemble the photo on your card; you don't want it to look like you are the mother or father of the person on the card! You also don't want to schedule a follow up meeting with someone and have the awkward situation where they don't recognize you because they're looking for the person in the photo. Authors are notorious for putting a twenty-year-old photo on their book cover and then they wonder why everyone asks where the author is at book signings.

If you network a lot, you will understand just how many people an active networker meets every week. A good picture goes a long way toward you being one of the few they remember. I get many compliments on my card. I have a photo on the back that is faded out. It's just enough where they can see me, but light enough that they can still write on it if they need to make notes.

I already mentioned this, but it bears repeating: don't clutter up your card! Keep it simple. All you really need is a logo (if you have one), your name, an email address, website address, and a phone number. There is no need to spell out the word "email", "phone" or "cell". People understand that already. You also don't have to write out "http://www." in front of a website address. You can simply use just the domain name itself, such as KathrynWheat.com. When they see the .com, or .net, they will know it's a website. Don't use up precious space on a card with these unnecessary characters.

Now let's address the idea that everyone likes referrals. We all do, but it doesn't really need to be stated on your card and I see this frequently. I personally don't like using up space on a card with catchy phrases, tag lines or anything else. They are only clever if they are truly unique, which few are. If you are using the same catch phrase that appears on thousands of other cards, it's just clutter and means nothing. You want to make sure it's worth taking up valuable real estate on your business card. Here is a photo of my card:

Front

Back

Always have easy access to your cards when meeting people. Men can usually keep them handy in a pocket. Ladies, if you carry a huge handbag, consider buying a nice cardholder to keep in your hand and leave the handbag at home or in the trunk of your car if that's possible. It's cumbersome and doesn't make a professional statement even if it is a beautiful designer handbag. Nobody wants to stand there waiting for you to dig around in your purse for ten minutes looking for your card and it's rude to expect them to do so.

As far as electronic cards go, I'm personally not a fan. I still don't see people embracing this technology on a widespread basis in the business world. Not even those in the tech industry seem to be using them, which is telling. Perhaps in the near future someone will develop an app that easily works with all phones but so far I haven't seen it. A good alternative is to take a photo of your card with your smart phone and text it to people. That way, they have a photo of your card with all the necessary information saved on their camera roll. Or better yet, ask the person who made your card to send you a high quality JPG and save it to your camera roll on your phone and/or computer.

If you are the kind that likes to make notes on people's cards, it's worth the money to invest in a nice looking pen. Don't pull out the pen you picked up from your insurance agent or your bank. Get one that is solid silver, gold or black. A sleek simple design is best. You don't have to spend hundreds of dollars to get something that makes a professional statement. Just don't pull out the plastic one with someone else's logo on it. Professionals do notice these things. Make sure you keep the pen handy as well. It makes for a less than glowing first impression if you appear disorganized. Networkers will be inclined to move on and talk to someone else while you are fumbling.

"The number-one
fear in life is public
speaking, and the
number-two fear is
death. This means
that if you go to a
funeral, you're better
off in the casket than
giving the eulogy."

~ Jerry Seinfeld

6

What's Your Opening Line?

I previously made reference to an "elevator pitch". I've already advised you about being naked and authentic. However, it is important to be able to talk effectively about what you do. You are networking to grow your business, right? So how do you navigate this necessary step of creating a short introduction about your business for networking and still remain genuine?

What does "elevator pitch" even mean? The term comes from the idea that if you found yourself on an elevator with the number one person that you've been trying to get in front of to pitch your product, service or idea, what would you say to get their attention in the time it takes for you to ride to the top floor in the elevator? I can promise you they won't be impressed with an overly practiced script. If you try to "sell" them anything, they'll see right through it. If they've reached the level of success that makes them the #1 dream person you are dying to do business with, then they probably get hit with "pitches" on a daily basis. They are more likely interested in who you are as a person and why you do what you do than by what you sell.

I don't even like the term "elevator pitch". You shouldn't be trying to "pitch" anyone or anything at networking events, which is why I prefer to say "introduction" rather than "pitch". The idea behind it is to be able to concisely describe who you are, what you do and how you can benefit the person you are speaking to and do so in a professional manner. The more prepared you are to talk about these things, the less likely you will be to let your nerves get the best of you and cause you to stammer or ramble on and on without clear direction or an end in sight. You must be able to introduce yourself to professionals and give them just enough information about who you are and what you do to intrigue them and leave them wanting more.

Remember, networking is all about starting conversations without a destination in mind. What you want to do is have enough experience talking about your profession that when you are presented with an opportunity to get in front of your dream client, you are not tongue-tied. That's a great reason to network! You'll get lots of practice and increase your business connections at the same time. People will ask you all kinds of questions about what you do. Over time, you'll find what creates genuine interest as opposed to what makes people's eyes glaze over while they fight the urge to run. Many times people are more intrigued about why you do what you do, than with what you actually do. Share your story. Tell people what made you want to get into the business you are in and follow where that path leads. Your story is your currency.

I mentioned Jim McInvale, founder of Gallery Furniture, a bit earlier and told how he started growing his business by doing silly commercials on TV. Another way that he's managed to grow his business is by telling his story. I've had an opportunity to hear him speak on three occasions and each time, he's told part of his story. The first time, he talked about how he and his wife came to Houston,

TX with nothing and he started Gallery Furniture with $5,000 and sold furniture out of the back of his truck. It's a true story of rags to riches. The second time I heard him speak, he talked about his daughter and her struggles with obsessive-compulsive disorder and how it's affected the whole family. The third time, he spoke about the fire that nearly destroyed his entire store. He didn't try to sell us on his store. He simply told his story and, with that, managed to motivate and endear all within earshot. Instead of presenting himself as the successful millionaire that he is and trying to impress, he showed up humbled and honest about where he'd come from and the struggles that he's faced. It allowed people to connect with him as a person.

For networking purposes, your introduction basically consists of a couple of sentences that tells a little about who you are and what you do. I'm going to show you how to create an irresistible introduction. A good one entices those listening to want to learn more. Again, don't be overly practiced and fake. If you aren't authentic, people will know. I have heard only a very small number of people effectively use slogans and rhymes in their introductions so I caution you to proceed carefully if this is what you want to do. This approach must fit your personality and feel authentic.

One of the most important things you must do is adjust your volume in order to be heard whether that is in a group or one on one. You need to be heard across the room if you are at a group meeting where people stand individually and make introductions. Make sure you speak up and project your voice or people won't even try to listen and you'll be ignored. This type of projecting takes some practice if you aren't used to it. This is something I've had to personally work on a lot. On the other hand, if you are speaking to someone one-on-one, adjust your volume accordingly there as well. If you notice people ten feet away looking at you, or the person you are speaking to steps backward perhaps you should turn it down a bit. Having someone shout at us is uncomfortable and makes us want to escape. Being too loud makes it difficult to listen so be self-aware and learn to adjust your voice.

You won't always present the same introduction to everyone. In group settings, where you see the same people on a weekly or monthly basis, they already know what you do. You shouldn't give the same introduction every time. They've heard it many times already. Consider changing it up each time. Start with saying your name, the name of your business and then give a motivational quote for the day or provide a helpful tip that pertains to your business. Remember that all the things that you know about your business aren't common knowledge to people outside of your field. You could even say something about a positive experience you had with another member of the group. The only time that you wouldn't start with saying your name is if you had some kind of jaw dropping quote, story or statistic that really grabbed their attention.

Vary what you say according to who is listening. It's important to be able to read the room and learn to comment on and compliment what others are saying as well. For instance, let's say someone is there from a local Italian restaurant, another person from a local bakery and even another person who is a personal fitness instructor. When you stand up to speak, you could mention each business and give them a boost. Here are a few examples of how you can do these things:

"Hi, my name is Kathryn Crawford Wheat. I'm a professional speaker, consultant, and author of the book, *Networking: Naked & Unafraid*. I think we need to sample some of the lasagna from Tino's Italian Restaurant. After that, some Italian crème cake from Bonnie's Bakery would be nice to finish off the meal. Then we'll all need to get in touch with Donny, the personal trainer. I suggest we schedule a group exercise class for our next meeting. If you want to know more about me you can go to <u>KathrynWheat.com</u>."

"Good Morning! Thank you, David, for organizing this meeting. My name is Kathryn Crawford Wheat. I'm a professional speaker, consultant, and author of the book, Networking: Naked & Unafraid. I like to share one of my favorite quotes from the late Zig Zigler, 'You don't have to be great to start, but you have to start to be great.' If you want to know more about me you can go to KathrynWheat.com."

"Happy Friday everybody! My name is Kathryn Crawford Wheat. I'm a professional speaker, consultant, and author of the book, Networking: Naked & Unafraid. If the thought of standing up and doing an introduction like this causes you to break out in a cold sweat, maybe we should talk. If you want to know more about me you can go to KathrynWheat.com."

"Hello, thanks for inviting me to visit your group! My name is Kathryn Crawford Wheat. I'm a professional speaker, consultant, and author of the book, Networking: Naked & Unafraid. My favorite networking tip is to start a conversation with no destination in mind. If you want to know more about me you can go to KathrynWheat. com."

"Hello, all! My name is Kathryn Crawford Wheat. I'm a professional speaker, consultant, and author of the book, Networking: Naked & Unafraid. I love the energy this group always brings to networking meetings. I want to give a shout out to Kathy, the bookkeeper. We had lunch last week and she told me about a great app to track my mileage when traveling for business. Everyone should schedule a meeting with her. She's a wealth of information. If you want to know more about me you can go to KathrynWheat.com."

"Did you know that I once rode an elephant in Taiwan? My name is Kathryn Crawford Wheat. I'm a professional speaker, consultant, and author of the book, Networking: Naked & Unafraid. If you want to know more about me you can go to KathrynWheat.com."

"According to a Cooking Light Insight Survey, only six percent of Americans get the recommended 30 minutes of daily exercise. I encourage you to get moving starting today! My name is Kathryn Crawford Wheat. I'm a professional speaker, consultant, and author of the book, Networking: Naked & Unafraid. If you want to know more about me you can go to KathrynWheat.com."

Notice there is a common theme. I usually start with my name, give a very brief description of what I do and then end with the name of my dot com which happens to also be my name. Take this basic outline and add to that your own greeting and message. You can include things that will benefit the people in the group, pose a question or problem you can help solve, state a startling statistic, share a fun fact, give a shout out to someone else in the group, provide a professional tip or favorite quote and you have an effective introduction that people will not only listen to, but will want to know more.

Here are a few examples of how different professions can incorporate business tips into their introductions:

- A Realtor could give tips regarding buying new versus existing homes.

- A financial advisor could give tips on how to maximize your savings.

- An insurance professional could give a tip on how to save on your insurance.

- An event planner could provide a tip on how to plan for food based on the number of RSVP's.

- Someone in the automobile industry could give a tip on leasing versus buying.

- A photographer could share a tip on natural versus artificial lighting for photographs.

- A tech guru could give an SEO tip.

The idea is to give valuable free advice to the people that you network with. They will appreciate your professional guidance and this will further enhance your personal brand equity and expert status in their eyes.

Usually there is a set time limit for giving introductions. Be prepared to stay strictly within the time frame. Whether it is 20 seconds or two minutes, don't ignore the guidelines. Time yourself and practice this a little bit! Just don't try to memorize a script or wing it. There is a gray area in between those extremes that is the sweet spot you should aim for. I caution you to not worry over this too much or stress yourself about it. When it's one of those situations where you are going around the room and everyone is waiting their turn, people are most likely not really listening to what you say anyway because they're thinking about what they are going to say when it's their turn or if they've already done theirs, they're worrying about how they sounded. So don't put too much pressure on yourself to get this perfect. Just be you!

Remember the story I told you about my first networking event and how nervous I was? Trust me; I didn't really hear a word anybody said. It wasn't that I didn't care. I was just too worried about what I was going to say. I was so caught up in trying to impress everyone and be like them that I was practically crippled with nerves. I hadn't learned yet that I must be authentically me, that I am enough. Be naked, be yourself and you won't have to be afraid.

The reason for the time limits is to make sure there is adequate time for everyone present to share their business with the group. If there is a timer, under no circumstance should you keep talking after the bell rings. This is one of my biggest pet peeves because several things are guaranteed to happen if you abuse the set time limit.

First, people will get extremely annoyed. Second, they will stop listening to what you are saying. All they are thinking about is that you are supposed to shut up! Third, if you had a few people intrigued with what you were saying before the bell sounded, you will lose more and more of their interest and respect with each second you exceed the time limit. I'm sure you've heard the phrase, "less is more", right? This applies to your introduction as well. More is not better, it's just rambling. Even if you are in the middle of a sentence when the timer sounds, stop what you are saying and state your name one last time and sit down. People will immensely appreciate what you did because when you exceed your allotted time, you are infringing on someone else's time and everyone knows it. Not to mention the fact that it's just plain rude! Don't do it! Ever! I mean never ever! I really can't stress this enough. Remember, the more you talk, the less people listen, especially at networking events.

Something to think about: I have a friend who stands up, states his name then he follows with a quote from his book, Miscellaneous Ramblings From a Slightly Deranged Mind, says the name of his dot com which is also the same as his name and he sits down. He doesn't even tell people what he does! Guess who everyone is crowded around at the end of the meeting? That's right. It's him! They are asking him what he does. Who has the power here? He does. He has people begging to know more. It never ceases to amaze me. They're all asking him what he does because he didn't tell them. The lesson here is that it's okay to leave people with a few questions. It's not necessary to tell everything about yourself on your first exchange. It's better to leave people with a few questions than to bore them with too much information.

I'm not recommending that you actually use this same strategy when starting out. Just because it works for one person doesn't mean it will work in every case. You have to have a certain presence, confidence and personality to pull off this type of thing. It works great for him, but it's not something everyone can use and it's certainly not an excuse to avoid actually speaking about what you do. I'm just making a point about how less is more.

When it comes to taking turns going around the room giving introductions, remember that most people are too preoccupied with thinking about what they will say when it's their turn to stand up to even really process what you say. This is a good reason to not get nervous about it. Just be naked and authentic and you will do just fine.

If you are still a bag of nerves after all I've said here, keep your introduction very short. If all you can get out the first time is your name, then just say your name and smile. It's okay! You won't get in trouble if you don't speak the entire allotted time. Think about my story of the first time I did this. I told you how nervous I was to speak in front of the room. Now I'm a professional speaker and instructor. I stand in front of rooms and speak for hours all the time now. I'm proof that it does get easier each time.

Give yourself permission to progress at a pace that you are comfortable with. Start with ten seconds and work your way up to a two-minute introduction. Never engage in self-sabotage by starting out apologizing for not being prepared or for being nervous. That will set expectations for failure and it is entirely possible no one will even notice how nervous you are. Nobody but you even knows what you are planning on saying so if you forget something it's not a big deal. Besides, you will be prepared because you've read this book and have learned how to give an irresistible introduction. For the most part, networkers are a nice group of people and they want to help you succeed. They had to start at the beginning too. They have all been right where you are and have felt those same emotions.

In case you are still wondering what a bad introduction sounds like, here are a few examples of what not to do:

There was a guy at an event that I attended who owned a patio furniture store that sold new furniture and also refurbished old furniture. He stood and proceeded to drone on and on about all the things they did to make chairs look new. First, you shouldn't go into that much detail about what you do during an introduction but additionally, it sounded a little X- rated as he went into a great amount of detail about strap on pieces and slings and things. Then he topped it off by saying the price was only $69! I'll just say that there were many people with their heads hung down avoiding eye contact with others and I heard suppressed snickers all around the room. I'm still not sure if he was aware of the double entendre of the words he chose to use but it didn't leave a positive impression.

Another example of a bad introduction is to get up and start going on about the great new product that you are introducing and how it's selling out fast and if everyone doesn't get one quick they are going to be gone, gone, gone! This is way too infomercially and pushy and will likely turn off everyone in the room.

Don't go into too much detail about what you do using industry jargon. This will have people tuning you out very quickly.

If you wear multiple hats and have several businesses, don't pull out 3 or 4 business cards from all the different businesses that you do and talk about each one. It confuses people. Be brief and allow people to come ask you questions when they want to hear more.

You should also avoid bad mouthing your competition under any circumstance, but especially if they are within earshot. One time I happened to be standing behind a woman who owns a local print and online newspaper in my area. She has always incorrectly thought my website was her competition. In reality, our markets are completely different. She had no idea that I was behind her, and could hear her, but she proceeded to tell the person she was speaking to that my website traffic wasn't nearly as good as hers and that they should advertise with her print newspaper because online marketing really didn't work. I turned around as I heard this and smiled at the person she was speaking to and walked away. The person she had been speaking to was a friend of mine and she gave me a sheepish grin and shrugged her shoulders. What an awkward moment this woman created by saying something so inappropriate! She made two crucial mistakes. First, she was putting the hard sell on someone and second, she was being disrespectful toward someone else and that person she was trying to sell knew it. Even if the person she was trying to sell hadn't been my friend, this tactic would have left a bad impression and the odds of her making the sale after that would be pretty much nonexistent.

When networking, you'll get asked all kinds of questions. What do you do? Why are you here? Who would you like to meet? What are your goals for your business? Yes, you must be able to answer these questions in just a few sentences. Notice I said, "Answer the questions." It's much better to wait for someone to ask about what you do than to start a conversation assuming they want to know. When you do get an opportunity to tell somebody what you do, don't hit him or her with a sales pitch. The idea isn't to attempt to sell something or get hired on the spot. Just start some conversations. Simply exchange information with people. Learn about each other. Ask other people questions.

Have genuine interest in people. They usually have remarkable and unique stories. They have insights and wisdom that can help you. We all have different experiences and learning from each other benefits everyone.

The more you can set a person at ease while talking with them, the more trusting and relaxed they will be toward you. Showing interest in the person will grow your business relationship to a much deeper level than superficial chit chat about the weather.

Ask them about their hobbies. Ask them why they got into the business they are in and how it came about. The key is to try to get past the guarded networker that is standing in front of you. Get to know that naked, authentic person underneath the polished exterior. It will help you decipher whether this is a person that you would like to form a lasting business relationship with or not.

I know a man who sells insurance. Now let's face it, unless you are in the insurance industry, talking about insurance is pretty boring for most people. Insurance is necessary but it's not something that we desire to have long meaningful conversations about unless we need to make changes to our own policies. A fellow networker asked him one time about what his hobbies were and he said he loved music trivia. It was suggested that he should start sharing some of his trivia knowledge at networking meetings. Now he talks more about music trivia and less about insurance and people relate to him much better. Yes, of course, he still tells people that he sells insurance and that he's there to help if they ever need him, but he also allows people to see that he's deeper (and more fun!) than an insurance salesman. He has become a much more interesting person by sharing a little bit about who he is, and what he likes to do, when he's not selling insurance.

Never, ever be the only one talking. Conversations aren't one sided. You don't need to tell people everything the first time you meet them. It never hurts to leave them a little curious! When people are ready to hear more, they will ask. When that happens, you are at an advantage, so wait and be patient. If they never ask, move on. They've just given you some very valuable information about themselves. They probably don't care about you or what you do. Don't waste your time with narcissistic people who never think to include you in the conversation and just expect you to listen to them. If you went on a first date with someone who droned on and on about how wonderful they are and proceeded to tell you all about their childhood, school, family pets, ex-lovers, and DNA profile and they never once asked you to tell them about yourself, would you want to have a second date with them? Of course not, you'd want to escape to the restroom and climb out the window and run!

I met a financial advisor once who approached me and introduced herself to me saying that she heard I had a website called Woman's InSite. She handed over her card and immediately went into how she wants to increase her female client base. Then she went on to tell me that I should connect her with everyone who is on my email list and my website so she can let them know all about how she wants to help women learn to let their money work for them, and on and on. She didn't even take a breath!

I'd just met this woman. Why she thought I'd be willing to turn over all of my contacts to her without even knowing her for more than two minutes is a mystery to me. Finally, I had to interrupt her and tell her I had to go. She never even asked me my name and the truth is that she didn't really care. She was so focused on trying to use me for my circle of influence that she neglected the most important part, which is to form a connection first. Needless to say, I didn't bother following up with her. No one likes feeling used so don't make this mistake.

"Great men are
seldom over-
scrupulous in the
arrangement of
their attire."

~ *Charles Dickens*

7

What to Wear?

Presentation is everything! How you present yourself says a lot to those you will be meeting. Make sure you aren't sending the wrong message! When it comes to wardrobe, details are important. If you are sloppy or inappropriately dressed, people will think you don't pay attention to detail or lack good judgment. Always dress professionally. By this, I don't necessarily mean that you must always wear a business suit. It's important to know your clientele and to dress for your profession. Take a good look at the successful people in your field and make note of their wardrobe. How they dress will give you an indication of expected attire for a professional in their position.

There are a few instances where a suit is called for. If you are a banker, business coach, financial advisor or another similar type of profession, you most likely need to wear a suit to a networking or any other professional event because people who hire or do business with those professionals have that expectation. You can absolutely still show your own style and personality but know that people will react to you based on how you present yourself. You can't really expect someone to come to your bank for a business loan if you show up to a networking event in sneakers and sweatpants! Ladies do have a little more latitude other than a business suit if you want to present yourself in a very conservative fashion. A dress with a cardigan or jacket will work as well. The main thing to remember is to be modest. This means necklines should be high and hemlines low.

Other professions can dress a little more causal. If you are a personal trainer for example, it's perfectly acceptable for you to dress for your business. However, don't show up in your workout clothes if you have just spent an hour sweating in them! We don't want to smell you before we see you. Just keep it neat and clean. If you are in a more creative field, dressing with a bit of flair is great! It will highlight your profession. The key is to dress appropriately for someone in your profession and it never hurts to lean toward the conservative side when networking, as the mix of professionals will include many professions.

Shoes are very important as they are our foundation and can make or break you, literally. If your shoes are pinching, rubbing, or causing you pain in any way, it will be noticeable. I have shoes that are good for a couple of hours but if I'm going to be out on my feet the entire day, they tend to become a huge problem. As the day goes on, your feet naturally tend to swell and those shoes that felt great at 8:00 a.m. can practically cripple you by 5:00 p.m. when you are heading out to a happy hour networking event. Make sure you test out new shoes before committing to them for the entire day. Sometimes, I'll even throw an extra pair of shoes in my car in case the ones I start the day in become uncomfortable. No one wants to talk to you if you are wincing in pain with every step. It's terribly distracting.

Also, pay attention to how your shoes look and what condition they're in. Men, a clean and shined pair of shoes makes a professional statement so take care of those scuff marks. Other men in particular will notice these things.

It seems obvious that your clothes should be clean but somehow there always seems to be someone at an event that doesn't understand what that means. If you spilled spaghetti sauce on your shirt at lunch and you live too far away to go home for a clean shirt, consider running by a store and buying a new one. You only get one chance to make a good first impression. Every event gives you the opportunity to meet someone who will take your business to the next level and that deserves your best effort.

Personal hygiene is also important. Make sure your breath is fresh. That doesn't mean to walk in chomping on gum to cover up the garlic you just ate. Breath mints are ideal. Many times you will be talking to people in close proximity. Take note if they are backing away from you and realize that your breath might be the issue. Make sure your nails are well groomed. Yes, this is for the men too. Dirty, jagged nails are a huge turnoff. I see this way too often! People do notice these things so pay attention to them.

Oh the dreaded bedhead! Do something with your hair so it behaves. I think men and women are equally guilty of this. I know a super sweet lady who I sat behind at one event and couldn't help but stare at the great divide on the back of her head. Her hair looked perfect from the front! I am always shocked to see an otherwise very smartly dressed person who has bedhead so don't forget to check all angles. You don't want to be remembered as the one with bedhead. Yes, people notice and it gives the impression that you don't pay attention to details. All of these things may seem small but when you put everything together, it can make a huge difference in how people perceive you. Even the tiniest detail can make a wrong impression. Like it or not, people DO judge you based on your appearance! You have the opportunity to make a good first impression so take charge of it.

If you aren't sure of what your style and brand should look like, hire a good stylist! It is well worth the money spent to get honest feedback from an unbiased person. They give you the honesty you really need. Don't count on your friends or family to tell you that you need a makeover. They're too close and don't want to hurt your feelings. Or perhaps they are used to you looking a certain way and don't want to see you change or even think a change is necessary. It may make them uncomfortable. Periodically hiring a stylist to keep your look current and professional is an ideal way to put your best foot forward when presenting yourself in a professional environment. Another thing a good stylist can do is help you understand how different colors affect how others perceive us whether we are here in the United States or among other cultures abroad.

Here are a few basics for colors in the United States and how they may affect people's mood or the impression they form about you:

Black: intelligence, authority, power, stability and strength.

White: purity, cleanliness, safety, and neutrality.

Gray: practical, timeless, or sometimes death or depression depending on the shade of gray.

Red: where the eye looks first, creates passion and excitement.

Blue: calming, dependability, wisdom, loyalty.

Green: growth, nature, money, peace, harmony.

Yellow: happiness, optimism but beware that bright yellow can cause tempers to flare.

Orange: fun, energetic, warmth and ambition.

Brown: reliable, stable, friendly, organic.

I remember several promotions that I did a while back for a plastic surgeon. He was always impeccably dressed and looked every bit the part of a successful surgeon. He was also quite personable so people were naturally drawn to him. He brought another doctor into his practice that was a bit younger and just beginning his career. While this younger doctor was attractive and personable, he had a sloppy haircut and wore outdated, ill-fitting suits. This added to his already boyish look. It wasn't a great first impression. He certainly didn't look like someone that you'd trust to be your plastic surgeon. I advised that he consult a style coach and even I couldn't believe the transformation. He now enters a room with style and presence and you know that he is someone you want to meet. He exudes confidence and success. A mature, stylish haircut and a new suit that fits correctly can make a huge difference on your first impression.

Now, let's talk a little bit about nametags. I really love nametags! There are several reasons why I suggest that you wear a nametag when networking. Many people are visual and seeing your name with your face helps them remember who you are. If you have a logo on your nametag, it also helps people remember your business affiliation.

If you network a lot like I do, you meet hundreds of people. You'll really appreciate seeing nametags on other people to help jog your own memory and help you with names of people you have previously met. Many times I'll run into someone that I know I've spoken with. I may even remember their business but their name temporarily escapes me. Seeing their name on a nametag avoids an awkward moment for both of us!

Remember the story I told you about walking up to the two ladies at the bar at the beginning of this book? After I recovered from my humiliation and embarrassment, I made my way into the crowd of people and realized that many people had on nametags and that was how I could differentiate between who was there to network and who was just enjoying an evening at the wine bar. Since then, I look for clues like nametags to help me know who to approach. If you have a nametag, those who want to network with you will approach you more frequently.

If you don't see a nametag, but still aren't sure if someone is at the venue to network, just ask him or her if they are there for the networking event. No big deal. Either they'll say yes or no. If the answer is no but they're nice, you still have an opportunity to meet someone that may end up being a great business connection. What's the worst thing that can happen? They laugh at you? It's okay. Laugh with them, it is kind of funny. Either way, you'll live through it. I did.

Many times there are temporary paper nametags available at networking events that you can write your name on and stick on your clothes. If you don't have a custom nametag, at least grab one of the temporary tags and use it. Then, at your first opportunity, get yourself a nice custom-made tag. It sends a message of stability and class. The temporary sticky tags tend to fall off and the next thing you know, people are walking all over your name on the floor! So do yourself, and others, a favor by making a small investment in a custom made nametag. I have a metal one with bling around the edges and a magnetic back so it cost a little more than a plain one but it has boosted my visibility tremendously when networking. Retailers such as Staples, Office Depot, Office Max, and Embroid Me are good places to check for pricing in your area. There are also many places online where you can order a good nametag and have it shipped to you. You can spend as little as $15 for a plastic one or a little more if you want something special. If you are ordering several for your company, then there will be a price break for ordering a larger quantity. I spent about $40 on mine.

"Humor results
when society says
you can't scratch
certain things in
public, but they itch
in public."

~ *Tom Walsh*

8

Manners Matter!

It can be difficult in the networking world if you are a single person. There are always those few individuals who will want to know exactly what you are selling and unfortunately they don't mean that in a positive way. This applies to both men and women. Dealing with interested individuals can pose some challenges and above all you want to be taken seriously as a professional. This means to dress modestly and conduct yourself in a way that is professional and establishes clear boundaries.

In my training, I've often been asked how to handle several different wardrobe malfunctions whether they are your own or they are with the person that you are having a conversation with. In the course of a day, our clothing tends to shift and we experience issues that can be embarrassing and send a not-so-professional message. Occasionally you are faced with an issue that another person has and may not be aware of. The question is how do you handle this in a professional manner? This can be a delicate matter, as you never want to lead someone to believe that you are looking at him or her inappropriately, especially in a business setting.

First, I urge you to be aware of your own clothing and how it may have shifted. Cleavage shouldn't be on display at all. You want to make sure you present yourself in a conservative and professional manner. If your blouse has shifted or your buttons are gaping, then make sure you rearrange your blouse and get a safety pin to close the gap. If your pants have a zipper, check your fly after visiting the restroom. Another problem with zippers is that when clothes don't fit properly, the material that is supposed to cover the zipper will bulge and gape open. This is a problem because the eye is drawn to the shiny zipper and it can be terribly distracting for the people trying to talk to you. It may not be clear if you have a problem with your fly being open or if your zipper is just showing. Someone that has just met you will not want to tell you that you need to check your zipper and will most likely not want to talk to you for long. They'll undoubtedly find a reason to walk away. It's best if you take care of the problem before others notice it.

I actually did tell a young man one time that he had a zipper issue and he grinned and said something about me looking. Because of this, unless I know you very well, I won't want to tell you. I try to remain professional. I don't want my comments to lead you to believe that I was intentionally looking. If you have zipper issues, trust me, people will not want to talk to you for fear of letting their eyes stray south. So if you sense that people are walking away from you and you can't figure out why, do a zipper check!

When wearing skirts, the practice of standing up and sitting down several times may cause your skirt to shift to the side or ride up. When you cross your legs it becomes a real problem. There are times that I've looked across the room at a networking event to see an otherwise modest lady whose skirt has fallen to the side and you can see all the way up her thigh when she sits down and crosses her legs.

I suggest that if you are wearing a skirt, do a mirror check before you leave home. What is a mirror check? Grab a hand held mirror, sit down in a chair, cross your legs and look in the mirror at what you may be putting on display for the person across the room from you. You may be surprised at what you see. Flowing skirts are the worst!

By all means, if a wardrobe adjustment is in order, please excuse yourself to the restroom. Falling bra straps need to be taken care of in private. Zipper checking, adjustments of private body parts or "junk jiggling" should also be taken care of in private. No handling the goods in front of fellow networkers, please! If we see you engage in this type of activity we don't want to network with you and we certainly don't want to shake your hand! I say this because I honestly believe that some people are completely unaware of some of their habits. Remember, your goal is to appear to be a professional and people are watching you all the time.

Once you have the clothing and personal hygiene addressed, there is the etiquette and manners required for food at an event. One thing to note about food that is served at most networking events is that unfortunately, it's usually not anything to write home about. If the food happens to be great, consider that a bonus. If it's bad, keep it to yourself. Complaining serves no purpose and will only make you seem negative. Keep in mind that your goal isn't to have a fabulous meal but to meet new people and grow your business. You are not there for free food.

By all means, if you do eat, display your best table manners. If you aren't confident about your dining etiquette, educate yourself! There are plenty of books out there that can help you. If you don't want to buy a book, there are tons of blogs and online resources that can guide you on proper dining etiquette. You can even hire an etiquette coach. If they have hors d'oeuvres and tiny little plates, they mean for you to only get one tiny little plate. Don't make a spectacle of yourself by acting like it's your last meal and piling your plate so high that food tumbles off. I've seen people do this too many times. Remember, you are there to make a good impression and that's a tricky thing to do when your mouth is full. Again, this is a time when less is more.

Also, never pile up food to take home with you! You would think this goes without saying, but I once witnessed a particularly brazen man stuff his pockets with food, fill three cups with coffee and then proceed to stack up and remove the small dishes that the snacks were served in. He was trying to juggle it all and get out the door when the host had to let him know that those serving dishes were not meant to be take-out dishes. His behavior created quite a spectacle!

If it's a happy hour, stand up type of event, eat with caution. It's extremely difficult to balance your drink, plate, business cards, and shake hands with business professionals all at the same time. If you must eat, move off to the side until you finish. Then you can move around and network without doing a juggling act.

There is one gentleman I know who is notorious for standing a little too close when he talks and, unfortunately, tends to spit as he emphasizes points. Add food to the equation and you get a firestorm of food particles flying at you. If you notice people backing up when you are talking to them, take the hint that something is putting them off! If it's a stand up event, my best advice is to not eat at all. Few people handle this tricky setting with grace and by avoiding the food; you also avoid the risk of embarrassment. Unless you are starving, skip the food. You are not really there to eat anyway. Do your networking and eat later.

It's much easier to eat at sit down breakfast and lunch events. If a presentation is being given you don't have to worry about talking while eating since you will just be listening. If it's the kind of event where you are eating but there will be a time for you to stand up and give your introduction, watch the progression around the room and prepare for your turn to come up. Stop eating a few minutes prior to it being your turn. This will give you a chance to grab something to drink and clean out your mouth before it's your turn to speak. Make sure you don't speak with food in your mouth. It's a huge turn off and makes the person across from you want to gag.

As you approach people and start to interact, realize that most business people will expect a handshake. Unfortunately, the art of the handshake seems to be getting lost in the age of cell phones which seem attached to the hands of people every second of the day. You need to put away your phone completely at a networking event so you can see who is physically in front of you and greet them. Having that phone in your hand may be comforting and familiar for you but it doesn't look like you are truly ready and willing to engage in networking if you are constantly checking your phone. Later we'll address the particulars of shaking hands in the proper way but for now just understand that you need to have your hands free. Unless you are expecting a call from someone needing directions to the venue, you should put your phone away for the duration of the event.

"The mark of a good conversationalist is not that you can talk a lot. The mark is that you can get others to talk a lot. Thus, good schmoozers are good listeners, not good talkers."

~ *Guy Kawasaki*

9

People are Talking!

In my classes, I often get asked what makes for good networking conversation and what subjects should be avoided. The idea of engaging in conversation with a total stranger can make some people nervous and unsure of what to talk about. Remember, you are there to start a conversation with no destination in mind. But what does that mean?

Good manners seem obvious most of the time but some things bear a reminder. It shouldn't have to be said not to engage in gossip while networking. This is especially true if you are talking about colleagues or people that you do business with. You really don't even want to be seen having conversations with people that are known to gossip. Like my mother always said, if they are talking about other people, they are most certainly talking about you, too. Just walk away and don't get caught up in any petty gossip. It is distracting, unprofessional and serves no purpose.

I knew two ladies who were business partners and professed to be best friends. Yet, they constantly threw each other under the bus and gossiped about one another. It was stressful to be around them. Each of them constantly tried to pull me aside and proceed to tell me all kinds of things about the other one that I really didn't care to know. I didn't know either one of them very well. They told me about marital affairs and all kinds of personal drama. Why on earth did they think I wanted to know all of their personal business? Whenever I tried to break away, they'd follow me. One even went as far as to intentionally leave the other out of photo ops. She would say, "Oh, let's take a picture real quick while she's not around!" I now avoid them both and I'm sure others they may have done business with avoid them as well.

There's also the lady who is constantly trying to run preemptive damage control. She gets into run-ins with other individuals on a regular basis and then tries to tell people her side of the story before they hear anything else. She assumes that the world is always talking about her conflict and starts talking about it as if everyone has already heard. Many times I have no idea what she's even talking about, nor do I care, it's just drama. Needless to say, I keep my distance from her because she's always looking for new drama, and she thrives on baiting others into her problems. I don't want to be her next victim.

These examples may sound silly and petty but, unfortunately, things like this happen more often than I even care to share. It is important to not only be aware of these types of time wasters, but to also prepare ways to extract yourself from their presence. Phrases like, "Good to see you again, but I must excuse myself. I really need to catch Mr. Jones before he leaves." Or, "It's been great to see you. I'm going to let you go for now." You can even make an introduction for them to someone they may not know and then leave the two of them to talk. These types of exits and phrases are polite but also great for getting away from obstacles like this and keeping your focus on positive networking encounters. Those in networking environments should understand that they are there to speak to many people so this type of exit isn't considered rude or blunt by serious business people. It's a very acceptable way to end a conversation and move on.

Once you have been to one or two networking events, you will start to encounter some of the same people. This is why it is important to talk to people about things other than your business. Get to know more about them especially if you see them on a regular basis. You are creating relationships and that means you know more about someone than just what they do. It also requires that you reveal more about who you are as a person as well. There are some people you will immediately click with and become fast friends. But keep in mind that you aren't there to only talk to people that you already know. While you want to create and maintain good relationships, at a networking function you have a goal of meeting new people.

When you think about meeting people, realize that they will not all be in the same industry as you. So by all means, please leave the industry jargon at the office. Use a layperson's language when talking about your job. You are not going to impress people with fancy acronyms and buzzwords. It doesn't make you sound smarter; it just confuses people and makes you seem insecure.

In the same way, don't assume that anyone wants to know about your certifications or degrees. If they're not in your industry, they are not going to be impressed with all the initials after your name. They have no idea what those certifications mean and really don't care. For instance, Realtors can take courses to become certified in many different aspects of Real Estate. With each certification or designation comes another set of initials to add to their business card. But that means nothing to those who are not Realtors. That's the kind of thing you need to tell your prospective clients about when they are considering hiring you, not the people in a networking environment. Trying to establish yourself as the most educated or smartest person in the room won't endear anyone to you. In fact, it will most likely create distance. Unless you are using networking to look for a job, people don't really want to get bogged down with the details of your education, job history or certifications.

Now when you think about starting a conversation with the people at a networking event, especially one you've been to a few times, figuring out what to say without sounding like a commercial can be a challenge. But here again, remember that you should not lead with your business. Instead, think of a few talking points that are trending right now, including newsworthy or current events. You don't have to talk business 100% of the time so don't limit yourself to a few narrow subjects as those you see regularly will get bored talking about the same old things all the time.

Don't forget that you shouldn't be the only one talking, so ask questions but make sure they are not closed ended – meaning they can be answered with one word. Rather, think of questions that are more open ended and require the person to explain or elaborate. For example, instead of saying, "Is this your first time at this event?" which can be answered with a simple yes or no, say, "Is this your first time to attend this event? Tell me what you know about it."

While you should talk about more than business, it is important to try to stay on topics that unify people. A good conversation starter is to ask people where they're from. People love to talk about where they grew up. It makes them feel at ease and most likely brings back good memories. You could make a positive comment about the venue or meeting to get the conversation going. You could ask if they know many people there. Maybe they know everybody and can make a few introductions for you or vice versa. While the goal is to get to know people, never ask someone you've just met questions that are too personal such as specifics about where they live or about their relationship status. This will put up their guard immediately and they will likely avoid you. If you get to know them, and become friends, then talking about more personal things will come naturally. Just don't jump into that too soon.

There are some other conversational pitfalls that you want to try your best to avoid. Certainly don't be the one that introduces unprofessional or negative dialogue into the flow as that is a conversation killer. These topics include anything that emotionally charges people such as race, religion or politics. Remember, when you talk politics, roughly half of the population is going to disagree with what you have to say on the subject. You should also steer clear of sexual innuendo, jokes or banter. If conversations like this do happen to present themselves then it's important to try to change the subject quickly. You could say something like, "This conversation seems to have taken a wrong turn somehow. Who saw the game yesterday?"

If you are in a large group of people and aren't successful in introducing a new subject then it's advisable that you excuse yourself and talk to someone else. There are some people that love to stir things up by bringing up these hot topics so it's wise to avoid them altogether. Others are aware of the penchant for drama these people have because most likely they've witnessed it first hand and will certainly notice if you seem to have a tight relationship with them and hang onto every word they utter. Even if you aren't responsible for introducing the subject matter, remember; you are judged by the company you keep.

Sometimes different languages become an issue with networking. We live in a multicultural world and many times languages other than the native English language are spoken. Use some common sense here. If you are networking in America, with English speaking people, you should speak English. If English isn't your native language, you may occasionally come across someone who speaks your native tongue and it's easier to revert to that language. That's fine if it's just the two of you who are talking. But if someone else is standing there who doesn't speak your language, it can be considered rude to suddenly start speaking in a language they don't understand. On the other hand, if you approach two people that are already engaged in conversation and you realize that they aren't speaking a language you understand, then you should move on. Don't expect them to stop their conversation and revert to English just for you.

If you are at an event where there is a speaker, or where people are invited to stand up and introduce themselves, don't talk or cause disruption at your table while others are speaking to the room. It's terribly distracting to the people at your table who are trying to hear the speaker. Also, if you must take a phone call, please step outside the room to talk. Don't kid yourself into thinking you are talking quietly enough. People hear you loud and clear. If you do talk on your phone during an event, you will be sure to make a less than favorable impression on those around you. I have witnessed people answer the phone at their table and proceed to hold a long conversation in the middle of a speaker's presentation. I have been tempted in the past to ask them to put the call on speakerphone so the room can follow the conversation better but, of course, no one wants to hear that any more than their one-sided conversation.

Don't Be Afraid: You're Ready!

"You need to bring something to the campfire. You need to thrive in the service to others. And you need to add new royalty to your kingdom at every turn. Access is the new aloofness. Inclusion is the new exclusivity."

~ *Chris Brogan*

10

Pick Your Crowd!

Now it's time to get out there and start some conversations. You have prepared for this by setting up your brand in a way that is going to give you an online presence and credibility. You have a killer business card. You know how to dress. You are prepared to give a memorable and effective introduction and your manners are in check. You've even brushed up on your conversation skills. It's time to put some of this knowledge to use.

You are ready!

I understand that the first event or two can be very nerve wracking. There are a lot of dos and don'ts to remember and no one wants to mess things up – I certainly didn't. However, when you have a thousand things running through your mind it can show on your face as a frown! You are concentrating on getting everything right so this is natural, but you still have to be aware that a frown is not what you want to lead with. The very first thing you need to do before walking into an event is to take a moment and put a smile on your face. Smiling will actually affect the way you feel on the inside as well as how you are perceived on the outside. Try your best to calm your nerves and have a confident approach. A good trick is to take a few deep breaths through your nose and blow out the tension through your mouth. You can even sneak into the restroom first and practice some power poses. A power pose is standing in front of the mirror and assuming the stance of your favorite super hero. Think about emulating Super Man or Wonder Woman. This will help your confidence level tremendously. If nothing else, it'll make you smile. Remember, I am basically a shy person and I promise you, it does get easier each time you go. You can do so much more than you realize. Just keep taking steps in the right direction.

Keep in mind that you can actually network everywhere, not just an event held specifically for that purpose. Anywhere you meet people is a good place to start a conversation. It can be at church, school, the gym, on the golf course, rotary club, running club, with your fantasy football buds or anywhere that you have an opportunity to get to know people. You never know where your best advocate or client will come from. Just be open to the possibilities everywhere around you and don't be afraid to talk to people about what you do. Many times we walk around taking care of our personal business in silence ignoring everyone and everything around us. Start conversations with the people that you see repeatedly in your everyday life. This can be great practice and will help you build the confidence to go to networking events. It's much less intimidating to start a conversation in line at the grocery store than at a large event so do it!

As far as organized networking goes, I encourage you to try out many different types of events. They can range from large conventions and chamber meetings to small luncheons consisting of only a handful of people. They all can benefit you so it's best to start by selecting the ones that you are most comfortable with. Keep in mind that you won't connect with everyone that you meet and that's okay. Like I said before, think of networking like you would speed dating. You will find yourself having many five-minute conversations at the beginning. Some you will want to continue, others you will want to politely move on. There's no need to be rude or to take offense either. You won't like everyone and everyone won't like you. This is not about selling everyone; it is about finding those few solid connections that will really grow your business. Don't worry about all the ones that aren't interested or that you will not connect with. One great connection is worth more than 50 so-so connections so keep that in mind.

Networking events can be broken down into four categories for the most part. There is the Breakfast meeting, the Lunch meeting, Happy Hour meetings and the larger type of events such as Conferences, Conventions, Seminars and Summits. Each type of event that you will encounter is unique in approach and style but all have their benefits. I want to encourage you to search for a few groups that you really like. Find groups where the energy, philosophy, or vibe is a good fit for you. Once you narrow down a few of your favorites, then consistently show up and become an active participant. This will create stronger bonds with the other professionals in the group, which leads to more genuine connections and better referral partners.

I have a friend who belongs to a networking group that has about 60 members and he has been attending their meetings every week for about six years. He has gotten more business and referrals from that group than any other group he has been in. This is largely due to his commitment to being present every single week. Consistency and follow through in attendance is a strong indicator of how you do business. People in your networking group will take notice of your habits.

Networking Group Type 1: Breakfast Meetings

Some people love early mornings, others, like me, not so much. If you are not a morning person, this might not be a good fit for you. These meetings get started pretty early, usually well before most people go to work. They tend to be more focused and serious about networking than any other type of group. After all, these business people get up early to start their day with networking. Typically there are fees associated with belonging to breakfast groups and with this type of group it is especially important to be punctual! These events usually start and end on time, as most have to get on with their day after the meeting.

Expect to stand up and talk about yourself for the allotted time. This can be your introduction that we talked about earlier. Respect the time limit given. Just remember, if it's the same people there every time, whether it's a weekly or a monthly meeting, you want to change up what you talk about. Think of giving some kind of tip that is related to what you do. You may want to share a motivational quote. Remember, always start with your name and end with your name. It helps people remember you and attach your name to your face. When the buzzer or bell sounds, say your name one more time and promptly sit down. Even if you are in the middle of a sentence, stop talking when your time is up. Just smile and say your name. I guarantee you; people will respect you for this.

Networking Group Type 2: Lunch Meetings

These types of meetings are also quite focused and structured. Again, there may be fees associated with joining and attending. Sometimes these networking lunches are called a "Lunch and Learn" meaning that there is some type of class or speaker during lunch. Typically, there is time for meeting and greeting others before the luncheon starts. You should always take advantage of this time. Your goal is to meet new people and greet those you already know.

If you can't get there for open networking prior to the meeting, it's important to arrive before the speaker begins so you won't interrupt them by walking in during their talk. It's very distracting to the speaker and to those trying to listen if you enter during the presentation. If you must leave early, sit near a door so as not to disturb the meeting in progress. Also, it is common courtesy to avoid having to cross the room during a presentation. You should be prepared to stand up and talk for one to three minutes at a lunch meeting depending on allotted time, which usually depends on the size of the group. Again, begin and end with your name and stop talking when the buzzer goes off! Really, I can't stress this enough! I see it all the time and it's a huge problem.

Networking Group Type 3: Happy Hour Meetings

These are a much more relaxed environment but they can be very productive if you approach it seriously. On the other hand, if you are just looking to have a drink or to make a love connection, go out with friends or join a dating service. This is not the time to flirt or drink too much. You will tarnish your reputation quickly if you aren't there for the purpose of making real business connections. You are not in the club to get tipsy!

Many times at happy hour socials and networking events, there is alcohol served. Sometimes it's even free. Don't be tempted by this. Know your limits! If people are asking you who is driving, that may be a clue that you've had too many. I suggest no more than one drink. It is not unusual for people to think they can hold their liquor better than they really can. If you get sloppy drunk, you will develop an unkind reputation and people won't take you seriously. Remember you are not there to lose business. You are there to grow your business. Networking isn't the place for a show of poor judgment by overindulging. Save it for the weekend if you want to test your alcohol intake limits.

Again, your goal is to meet new people and greet those you already know. Be careful not to spend all of your time hanging out with the same group though. It's important to work the room by circulating around and meeting as many people as possible. I first try to find the host and thank him/her for the event. You may want to ask the host about who is there in case there is someone that they think you should meet. I have had quite a bit of success with this method. Then as you circulate, briefly greet friends as you look for new people to talk to. This becomes easier after you've attended an event a few times because you will become familiar with the regulars and can quickly discover the new attendees. As you approach a new person, smile and speak with purpose when you introduce yourself. Start with a greeting and say your name as you extend your hand. Ask for their name if they don't offer it right away. They may assume you already know their name, or they may be nervous and just not realize they haven't given you this basic information.

As you develop business friendships, try going with one of these friends or meeting them there so they can be your advocate and you can be theirs. If you periodically separate and then reconnect as you each circulate, you can introduce each other to people that might be a good fit. You can also help each other out by telling new people about one another's business and accomplishments. Happy hour events are usually free and rarely have a speaker so expect to mix and mingle on your own. There usually won't be an organized meeting and this is great for good networkers, but not so great if you remain a wallflower. If you are really new to networking, you might start with the more structured meetings and work up to a happy hour get together once you have more confidence in your networking skills.

Remember to look for people wearing nametags. It will be up to you to introduce yourself and start conversations. While there is no question that this can be intimidating for those new to networking, I have met some great people at these events and I urge you to give them a try. If you are unsure of yourself, walk in with the goal of talking to at least three new people. You can do that. I suggest that you arrive early for these events. The most serious networkers will be there first and will leave before the wild ones start going beyond the acceptable limits in terms of alcohol, conversation or anything else.

Networking Group Type 4: Conferences, Conventions, Seminars, Symposiums and Summits

Typically there is an entrance fee for these. I will say that this type of event can be overwhelming if it's a large group, or if it's your first event. I would certainly recommend you get some experience at smaller events first just to take the pressure off. Even if you choose a large event as your first try, don't let it intimidate you. Your goal is not to meet everyone there – it's not about quantity, it's about making quality connections. Just start talking to people and move along quickly if it doesn't seem like they are someone that you connect with. Most exhibitors are eager to talk to you, as they are there to tell you all about their product or business. For this reason, you may have to extract yourself from the "pitch" on occasion, especially if that person doesn't understand how not to lead with their business. Remember, it's perfectly fine to exit the conversation by stating that you are making the rounds or that you have someone across the room that you are going to meet. You do not have to allow someone to monopolize your time just to be polite.

If you are shy, consider becoming an exhibitor. That way, you will be in a position where people will be approaching you. This makes it much easier to engage in conversations in this type of environment because only those interested in what you may have to offer will approach. Just keep in mind, you'll be somewhat stuck in your booth and won't have an opportunity to make the rounds unless you have someone helping you that can man your booth if you decide to get out to circulate.

If you are an exhibitor, you must understand that your time is limited. Be aware of the attention hog that will try to monopolize your time as other people approach your booth. You need to be able to juggle speaking to several people at once before you sign up as an exhibitor as this can really take some skill. Ideally, you will greet each person that comes to your booth but sometimes it just doesn't happen that way and you will get swamped on occasion. It is great to have help manning your booth to engage those people until you have a chance to chat with them and also to talk to people if you want to circulate the exhibit hall or just need a break.

Now that we've gone over the main types of networking events, let's talk about exclusive groups. You will hear this term on occasion when people describe a networking group to you. If a group is exclusive, it means they only allow one member from each type or sector of business. For instance, there is only one Realtor allowed in the group, one graphic designer, one dentist, one business coach, and so forth. There are pros and cons to this type of arrangement. Some types of businesses are heavily represented in the world of networking such as real estate, insurance, and financial advisors so it can sometimes be difficult to gain membership in an exclusive group.

Also be aware that in many exclusive groups you are expected to make referrals to only the people in your group and if you don't, it can create problems. Many networkers have an issue with this, as do I. What if your best friend is a Realtor and you have recommended him or her to your friends for years? If that Realtor friend isn't in your group, you aren't supposed to recommend him or her to your network. You are supposed to only recommend the Realtor in the exclusive group. If you don't, it can even be grounds for removal from said group. In fact, in some of these exclusive situations, you can also be removed from the group if you don't make enough referrals to group members or you miss too many meetings.

I'm not saying don't join an exclusive group, but just know what you are getting into. Your business may grow much faster if you make connections with many, many business owners, even many from the same profession; so don't limit yourself unless you feel you are really getting a huge benefit.

A major part of your value as a professional networker is tied to who is in your personal network. You are providing a valuable service to people when you connect individuals within your network. Anytime you have an opportunity to tell someone about another professional that can benefit him or her, it's a win/win situation for everybody involved. I personally don't care for exclusive groups that require a certain number of referrals. I like to make referrals to whomever I choose without it being regulated by a group that I belong to. What if I don't even like the Realtor in the group? If you choose to join a group that requires referrals, make sure you are comfortable making referrals to everyone in the group. Keep in mind that your reputation is at stake when you refer someone. You are standing behind them saying that this is a person that can be trusted and is a professional that you would personally hire. This shouldn't be taken lightly.

On the other hand, one of the benefits that comes from belonging to this kind of group is if you are just starting out or trying to break into a new market and want to grow a network quickly, joining a group like this will get you some referral business fairly fast.

As I previously mentioned, for the purposes of this book, I'm mainly speaking about organized networking groups and the events in terms of where they meet but these are by no means the only networking opportunities you should explore. Keep in mind that you can actually network wherever you are active. You can start a conversation just as easily on the golf course or in the bowling alley as you can in an organized group. If you participate in community activities, in clubs or volunteer at your child's school, make sure you let people know about your business. You never know where you might make a great connection. Your son's Boy Scout leader may turn out to be the CEO of the company where you've been trying to get your foot in the door.

One time I was shopping for a dress to wear to an event that I was hosting and the clerk asked if I was buying the dress for a special occasion. I could have just said yes and nothing more but instead, I told her about my website and the party I was having. The lady in the line behind me asked some questions about what I did and eventually asked for one of my cards. She is now a totally devoted fan of my website. If I hadn't told the clerk about my website, that lady in line may not have ever heard about it. Whenever you get an opportunity to talk to people about what you do, take advantage of it and don't let the moment pass.

I also want to take a moment and caution you about joining groups that require a fee, not because you shouldn't join one, but because you should ask some questions first. Such as, where does the money go? Is it a nonprofit? Is it going into someone's pocket rather than supporting future events? Is it a type of pyramid where an individual buys into a group and then has to pay another person to use the group name? How many levels of people are getting paid in order for you to be a member? What are these people actually doing for that money? Keep in mind there can be a great deal of work that goes into maintaining a lively and productive networking group.

Maybe the fee isn't very much and all the money goes toward throwing a huge party at the end of the year. Just ask questions and have a clear understanding about where the fees go. There are some very good groups that are valuable enough to pay to be a member of, but choose wisely because you can network yourself into the poorhouse if you don't pay attention to how much money you are spending versus the benefit you are gaining. In addition, joining every group you visit does you no good if you don't have time to actively participate in them.

Take a close look at the true cost and calculate how much you are actually spending. Is there a fee to join? Is there a fee to park? Are you driving on toll roads to get there? Are there mandatory meals to be purchased? What about meeting fees? Do they strongly "encourage" participation in raffles? Are you expected to donate a door prize? You can easily be nickel and dimed into well over $1,000 per year in some groups. If you do stay in such a group, make sure it's working for you and your return on investment is several times the cost. Also take into consideration whether or not you see the same people at other events that are free. If that were the case, why would you pay to sit in the room with them for a fee? The fee isn't gaining you access you wouldn't otherwise have and for me that is really the determining factor. You have to get something for your money that you can't get for free.

I joined a breakfast group one time that had a minimal annual fee. A red flag should have been that they required an application with three references to people that I've done business with along with all kinds of other information. It seemed a bit much for a local networking group. It almost felt like I was filling out a job application! I had been attending meetings for several months when they decided to change the rules on purchasing breakfast at the meeting. While it had been optional when I joined, they decided to make it mandatory. The cost of breakfast made for a 500% increase in the cost to be in the group! Needless to say I was not amused at their bait and switch technique and subsequently left the group. I'm not a morning person anyway and this was the final straw for me. I had paid for a full year but was only in the group for three months. I still lost the full amount so make sure you understand all the rules upfront, including their refund policy, before joining any fee-based group.

"The secret of getting ahead is getting started."

~ *Mark Twain*

11

Let's Get Started!

Now is the time to get out there and test the waters in this new world of networking. The good news is that most groups that require memberships will give you at least two visits before you have to join so you can get started right away without any investment at all. In the beginning, visit as many different kinds of groups as you can before deciding if you want to join anything. Again, don't ever visit a new group thinking you will make a sale on your first visit! It's not that I'm being repetitive; it is just that this is one of the most common mistakes I see each and every day and don't think that seasoned networkers don't occasionally do this too! Please don't lead with your business and pressure people.

Start conversations and try to keep an open mind. When visiting a group for the first time, be especially careful with your introduction and don't make it sound like you are giving a sales presentation to the room. Networking is about developing relationships. It's not about getting a quick sale. You'll make a really bad first impression to the group if you are pushy or try to dominate every conversation.

Understand that it takes time before people will get to know you and trust you. Also, don't introduce yourself to everyone and then leave during the speaker's presentation. This gives the impression that you think you are too important to listen to another person's presentation and are just in the group to sell, not make connections. Be gracious to the host, enjoy the meeting and always say thank you!

It's important to move around and mingle during meet and greet opportunities before and after an event or at Happy Hour events. Don't plop your rear end down in a chair and expect people to come to you. Be open and available! When you sit down during a time when people are meant to mingle, it sends a message that you are not interested in talking to others – and they won't approach you.

Also remember not to just hang out with your friends or business contacts you've already made here or elsewhere. You are there to meet new people. All too often I see people who work together come into an event and spend the whole time hanging out together never meeting new people. They may as well just go have lunch or drinks together and catch up on office gossip. That's what they're doing anyway and at least other networkers won't witness their cliquish behavior. If you are going to go, remember why you are there and make it productive.

I love networking and have attended many, many events, but everything must be done in moderation. I want to caution you about over committing yourself to networking because it is so easy to do. Yes, there can be too much of a good thing. I have attended as many as four events in one day and I'd say that's too much for me. I didn't even care to have a conversation with my own children after that day! You will have to set your own limits. At some point, it becomes difficult to remember who you have met and how you want to follow up. If your brain is foggy from having too many conversations, it defeats the purpose of being there.

Don't worry about how to find out where **all** the networking is going on. Once you start networking your name will get added to many invite lists and many event hosts will find and invite you! Often at these events there is a bowl where business cards are collected and if you drop your card in, you will be put on the invite list for all future events. You can also ask people that you connect with where they like to network. Most people are happy to share networking opportunities with others. Once you start going to events, your name will get added to many networking groups in your area and you will have invitations to join on a daily basis.

MeetUp, Facebook and LinkedIn are great social media sites to look for networking opportunities in your area. Find a specific type of group using search terms. For example: if you are a Realtor, you can enter in the search criteria "Real Estate" and the name of your town or zip code. You can also do an online search for networking groups in your industry. For example, if you were an engineer, you would search the words, "engineer networking events" along with your zip code or town. I live in the Houston area so I would search the exact words "engineer networking events Houston". That will bring up different events and groups for where you live. You can also check into the local Chambers of Commerce. They are usually great places to get plugged into what's going on in your region.

The practice of the RSVP (repondez s'il vous plait) has become lost in the onslaught of virtual invitations. I personally get bombarded with invitations via text, Facebook and email on a regular basis. On top of that, what is really an opportunity for people to sell their stuff has become disguised as a party so it makes it difficult to tell the difference unless you ask some questions first. Usually these are direct marketing sales events where they either expect you to buy a product or join their business. I get this type of "party" invitation all the time. Because of this increased practice of calling a selling opportunity a party and inviting thousands of people, many people have just stopped giving a reply to anything. I don't feel it's necessary, or even possible, to RSVP to these types of selling opportunities so I don't.

However, inaccurate RSVP's, or a lack of them, makes getting accurate head counts very difficult for hosts of more traditional types of events like luncheons and seminars. They need to plan for food and space requirements. I've noticed a trend of some people replying yes to everything just so their name will be seen yet I never see them show up to anything. If you RSVP to a traditional networking event where food is being ordered for you, then your reply needs to mean something. Don't be one of those people that RSVP to everything and show up for nothing because people will notice and infer that you don't follow through on what you commit to. Your word should mean something.

Always respect traditional mailed invitations and if you reply that you will be there, then be there. In these days of virtual everything, common courtesy sometimes gets lost and you want to be the person they remember in a good way, not the one that never shows.

Don't be afraid to try new groups, but get some information before you go. There are some eccentric groups out there, but there are even more fantastic ones to be discovered. Just remember to ask questions about the group's focus and try to get a reference from someone whose opinion you value and who has attended the meetings. If you are still not sure about the group, have a good exit strategy before you walk in. Announce that you can only stay a short time and sit near the door so you can slip out if necessary.

"Nothing is a waste
of time if you use the
experience wisely."

~ *Rodin*

12

Seasons

There are actually different seasons to consider when networking. The very busiest and most lively time of year to network is January through April. In January, many people are launching new businesses and are anxious to meet new people. If you are a beginner to networking you'll fit right in because there will be many newbies in the crowd anxious to make new connections. You can work through figuring out your networking strategies together and you won't feel like the only one in the crowd that doesn't know everybody.

Another thing that happens in January is that in the beginning of a New Year, many seasoned networkers look at their networking habits from the previous year and commit to making more connections in the upcoming year. It's kind of like a New Year's resolution for business. Business people approach the New Year with a renewed sense of determination and purpose for their businesses just like they do in their personal lives. They set goals and do their best to stick to them. Whether it's the veteran networker or the newbie, there will be well-attended events everywhere you go and lots of new people to meet. Just like with personal New Year's resolutions, as the months pass by, sometimes the commitment starts to fade and people will drop off. By March and April, you'll notice a lower attendance rate, as only the most serious networkers will continue with their commitments.

Starting in May, many people with school age children get temporarily sidetracked with end of year school programs. There are graduations, band programs, athletic banquets, and all sorts of recognition celebrations that will be taking networkers away from their regular schedules. Then summer starts and family vacations are taken. For these reasons, May through August tends to be much slower with very light turnouts to events. It can still be a good time to network though. The crowds will be much smaller so it's a good opportunity to stand out more. Use this time to solidify connections you have previously made. Get to know the people that are there even better.

Once school gets back in session, September through mid-November can be quite productive. Most events are very well attended during these months. Many networkers that had been absent over summer months get active once again with a renewed sense of purpose. They are trying to get back out there and re-connect before the craziness of the holiday season starts.

November and December are the lightest months of activity when it comes to true networking but there are still many holiday parties to attend where you can strengthen previously made connections. Try to get out as much as possible during this busy time of year. If you can, make the rounds at holiday parties so you can meet a few new people and solidify previously formed relationships and spread good cheer. This can be exhausting, so remember to know your limits. Don't network more than you can manage as far as follow up. If you don't have time or energy to touch base after meeting new people then it defeats the purpose of meeting them in the first place.

If you are just starting out, don't fall into the trap of waiting for the New Year. Go ahead and connect with some people in November and December when the groups are small so you will have built up your confidence when January comes along and numbers of attendees increase.

"Manners are a sensitive awareness of the feelings of others. If you have that awareness, you have good manners, no matter what fork you use. "

~ Emily Post

13

A Few Tips

Once you decide where you want to go, here are a few more tips that will help you. I know I've compelled you to be authentic, and naked, but there is one thing that is okay to fake. That is confidence! Even if you are nervous about visiting a new group, fake it till you make it. This is not just a saying. In order to have confidence, you must project that confidence even if you aren't feeling it. No matter what we are doing, if we grimace, we send a message to our brain that says this is difficult. On the other hand, if we smile, we send a message to our brain that says this is okay; I'm comfortable with this. Confidence upon entering a room makes all the difference in the world. Think happy thoughts, practice your power pose, hold your head up, and walk in like you own the place. I promise, no one will ever know if you are shaking like a Chihuahua on crack on the inside. If you are feeling butterflies in your stomach, realize that this is your body's normal process to prepare for projecting more energy, which is needed when we are in social environments. Make those butterflies work for you! After you've conquered your nerves a few times, it will become easier to do so the next time.

Once you begin attending multiple events, you will notice some of the same people that you see at other events. If you become uncomfortable or nervous, retreat to a familiar face and reconnect for a while. Just don't stay there in your comfort zone the whole time. Allow yourself a few minutes to regroup. Mentally tell yourself you can do it, and then force yourself to go meet someone new.

Don't forget to look for nametags if you are having a hard time determining who is there with the networking group. If it's in a restaurant, ask the hostess where the group is meeting so you don't have to wander around looking. If it's in a hotel, ask at the front desk or look for a small marquee with details for the meeting room.

Many times if you look around, you'll see that you are walking in with someone just like you who is also looking for the meeting. Ask if they are here for the meeting and figure it out together. This can be your first contact and who knows, maybe a longtime ally in the networking community. I will tell you that it is not unusual to make a mistake right off the bat and walk into the wrong room or get off on the wrong floor in a building. Don't let it shake you. Take a moment, along with a deep breath, and then put that smile back on your face before you enter the event.

One time I was driving around trying to locate the venue for a networking party and my map kept sending me to a residential neighborhood that I knew wasn't the correct location. I was getting frustrated and pulled over to take a better look at my GPS when I noticed another car was circling the same area that I was in. I could tell the lady in the car was lost too. Finally, I put down my window and asked her if she was looking for the same location and event. She laughed and said yes, she was driving in circles too! We ended up following each other and eventually made it to the event we were trying to find. We are now friends and continue to get a chuckle about how we met.

One you become familiar with a group; look for people standing on the periphery during a meeting. These individuals tend to be shy or more introverted people. They are also probably new and nervous. They will be thrilled that you have come to talk to them. If you aren't the shy type, then be aware of others who are struggling. Everyone was new once. Help them out by introducing them to people that you already know. They will deeply appreciate your kindness and remember you. You'll become known as a connector, which is a good thing to be as everyone will know you or want to know you.

One other tip, and it really goes back to conversational etiquette, is that when you are speaking with someone, be present in the conversation. Don't constantly look over the shoulder of the person you are talking with searching for someone else to talk to. Make eye contact and listen to what the other person is saying. People will notice if you are only listening in a halfhearted manner.

If you are standing and having a conversation with someone, stand in a way that leaves an opening for others to walk up and join your conversation. Pay attention with your peripheral vision. Be open to people. Don't close in the ranks if you see someone approach. Sometimes I people watch at networking events and it never ceases to amaze me when I see someone approach a group of people who are talking and they get completely shut out. I don't necessarily think this behavior is intentional. People just don't pay attention so be aware of what's going on around you. You are there to meet people, not to have private conversations.

On the other hand, if you are the one trying to join a conversation, be patient and wait for an opening. Don't walk up to a group and interrupt people who are talking so you can introduce yourself. Never thrust your hand into a person's face when they are in the middle of a conversation. Stand there a minute and try to get an idea of what is being talked about. If they are hashing out a business deal, then it's not a good time to try to connect. Keep moving. The whole idea is to be sensitive to what's going on.

If you are holding a drink, I suggest that you hold it in your left hand. That way, when offered a handshake, your right hand is free to shake hands and it's not cold and wet from the glass. That doesn't make for an ideal first impression. This seems like a small thing, but first impressions come and go very quickly. Think ahead and make sure you are doing all that you can to make it a good one.

Make the effort not to sit on the edge of the room with your back to everyone as it gives the impression that you are antisocial or cliquish. You may think you'd never do it, but we all do on occasion. It's easy and comfortable, especially if you are feeling nervous. And by all means, don't be exclusionary or unaccepting if someone approaches you for conversation. Even if you have been in business for 20 years and have that MBA or PhD remember that there is always more to discover and learn. Maybe that young graduate can give you some insight to new developments in your field that you may not yet appreciate or perhaps they can connect you with a younger market that you may need. ***Starting conversations is the whole reason you are there!***

"My belief is that during conversations, it's not so much what you say; it's how you say it that matters. What's being heard is secondary to what's being seen, as body language leads the discussion and dictates the mood. "

~ *Jarod Kintz*

14

Body Language

If you think about it, we start reading body language from birth. When we are infants, we begin to recognize the smile and soft eyes our mothers show us as unconditional love. As we grow up and start to disobey our parents, we learn the look of disappointment and know when we have crossed the line and are in trouble without a single word being spoken. We store all the information we gather as we go through life and recognize repeated facial expressions and gestures. We think we just get a vibe or instinct about someone but usually it comes down to their body language. We are drawing conclusions about them from years of data stored in our memories.

Watching how others interact with the people around them will tell you a great deal about them as people, but understand that people are watching you as well. Words don't matter nearly as much as actions! Once you get out there and start networking, people will see you everywhere! That includes in your car, in the grocery store, at restaurants, virtually anywhere you go you may be recognized. If you pull into the parking lot of a networking event blasting your horn at the person in front of you who forgot to use his or her blinker, it's almost guaranteed that someone you know will see you. Or, you'll park your car and see this same person walk into and attend the same networking event that you are headed to. Yes, you are being watched and people are always making judgments about your behavior! How you conduct yourself when you think no one is watching tells us who you really are.

A great deal of communication can take place without a single word being spoken. A study on body language conducted by Albert Mehrabian revealed that only 7% of communication is verbal or the actual words being used, 38% comes from tone, and 55% comes from facial expression or body language. It's up to you to make sure you are sending the right messages and that you understand the signals being conveyed by others. Following are a few basics, but you can find a great deal of detailed information in various books, videos and online blogs pertaining to specific situations and what certain body language may reveal to others.

Many times we unconsciously mirror the body language of people we are talking to when we want to bond or establish a rapport with them. If you notice that a person is mimicking your body language, they are forming a connection with you.

If someone is standing physically close to you, they are thinking of you in a warm way. However, if you notice that when you move toward them, they take a slight step back, they are uncomfortable with you or something you are doing. Also be aware that different cultures have different boundaries for personal space, as do different individuals. One way to discern the correct space is to watch how they stand in relation to others.

Be careful of creating any kind of barrier between you and other people. This can be anything from crossed arms, holding a large handbag in front of you to holding onto papers or even a glass directly in front of your body. It puts something between you and other people and will make you seem less approachable.

Face touching or scratching the back of the head or neck usually indicates that someone is lying, especially when touching the nose. When someone covers his or her mouth when speaking, it usually means they are telling a lie. Stroking the chin means someone is making judgments or decisions about what you are saying. Try to keep your hands away from your face.

Picking at the clothes and looking down usually means that someone is not in agreement with what is being said but wants to remain silent about his or her opinion.

When someone has their hands on their hips or rests their hands behind their head or even reclines in this position, they believe they have the upper hand. It can be a position of challenge and arrogance.

Slouching gives a signal of low self-esteem. Stand with your shoulders back and chest out to look and feel more confident. Think about power poses.

When networking, if a person's torso and feet are slightly angled away from you during conversation, it usually means they are open to others joining in the conversation. When we are fully engaged in a conversation or if it is private, we directly face the other person.

Chair straddling signifies a person who wants to demonstrate dominance while at the same time be protected.

Standing where hands are clasped at the front of the body over the genitals is a protective stance while hands clasped behind the back is one of confidence. Hands in the pockets show discomfort or mistrust.

I've given you a few examples of body language but it is not a hard and fast science. These actions I've mentioned don't always mean something, but they are clues for you to put together with the context in which they are used. As time goes along you will gain experience picking these things up so you have a better idea how a conversation is being perceived and if a person is, or is not, connecting with you.

"Don't act like a gunslinger whipping your card out of your pocket as you approach someone ready to fire. "

~ Kathryn Crawford Wheat

15

Get Carded

You wouldn't think I would need to spell this out but here goes: bring your business card! I know I mentioned it before, but you wouldn't believe the number of people I meet at networking meetings who "forget" to bring business cards. I've had people confess that they actually do this on purpose so they can be in control of collecting other people's cards instead of giving out cards, which seems a little ridiculous to me. They act like they don't think most people are worthy of receiving their card or that they want to cherry pick the options and not deal with people who they feel are beneath them so they don't bring any or they keep just a couple of cards stashed away in case someone comes in that they are impressed by. This is silly game playing in my opinion as if they believe that they are the crème of the crop and above normal networking etiquette. Just be present and be genuine. If someone is really weird and freaks you out, of course you don't owe them a card. But let's get real here. That almost never happens!

Let me be crystal clear, the idea isn't to lead with your business card so please, don't act like a gunslinger whipping your card out of your pocket as you approach someone ready to fire. Introduce yourself first, not your business. Ask people about themselves and their business. Usually that leads to them asking you about yours. If they don't ask, no problem! Tell them thank you and move on. You never know what's going on with people. They may be self-centered or maybe they are just saving you a little time by letting you know that they don't see a good connection with you. Or maybe they know they are about to be promoted to a position where they wouldn't be the contact person for what you are looking for and aren't permitted to announce this yet. Don't make assumptions.

I met a man from networking who told me that he wanted to become an instructor with my real estate school. We spoke several times about what was needed to get this set up and I sent him all the necessary forms for his review. Six months went by and he didn't act on any of it but kept telling me that he was serious about doing it. I didn't badger him about it when he brought it up but I did wonder why he hadn't proceeded with getting his certification. With a little patience on my part I eventually understood why he needed to wait. It turned out that the bank he worked for, and was being sponsored by, was being bought out by another bank and he wasn't at liberty to divulge this information. Once the buyout took place he moved forward with all he needed to do to get his teaching certification and course approval in place. So never assume you know what is going on in someone's life.

Once you have established some dialogue, decide if you would like to keep in touch with this person and if you do, ask them for a card. Don't immediately stick it in your pocket or drop it into your purse. Take a moment to look at their card! Respect it! Read what's on it. Ask them questions about anything of interest on the card. Don't immediately put it in your back pocket or drop in into that huge handbag. Please don't use it to pick your teeth. I'm sure you would never do this, but there is a reason that I mention it. Yes, I've actually watched people do it.

You will also notice cultural differences as well in the way people treat business cards. Asian people will almost always hand you their card with both hands with their fingertips holding the upper corners on each side. When you hand them your card you will notice how respectfully they receive it. Take note of these things and return the favor with the same respect.

Your reason for connecting doesn't have to be strictly for business purposes. You may meet people that you just think are interesting. While you may not immediately see how you will do business with them, you never know who they may know. Good connections aren't necessarily someone that you will make a sale to. You may be able to learn something from them. Maybe they will become a great advocate for you. It certainly never hurts when you have tons of people telling others about your business and how great you are even if they haven't ever bought anything from you themselves.

Don't hand out your card without having a conversation with someone first. I remember one event that I went to where a lady walked around the room handing out her card to everyone without saying a single word. She didn't say hello or introduce herself in any way. Afterward, I overheard her saying that she couldn't stay for the whole event. She just wanted to make sure everyone got her card and then she left. Guess where that card ended up? That's right, in the nearest trashcan that I could find! I have also seen people go around the room before events and leave a small pile of cards on each table trying to ensure everyone gets one. Guess where they were after the event – that's right, on the table right where they were placed. What a waste of their resources. It didn't do much for their personal brand equity either.

I'm assuming that we all pay to have our cards printed. They're not free! The idea isn't to get rid of them as fast as possible so you can buy some more. Be prudent with them and judicious with how you present them. Wait for someone to ask you for your card. Don't just assume they want one. Business cards should be used as a tool to connect with people and not as pieces of paper that end up as litter someone had to clean up or filler in a trashcan. Ask others for their card. Take notes on the back of it if necessary to remind yourself when and where you met that person. Usually, if you ask for someone's card, they will in turn ask for yours. If they don't ask for your card, don't give them one. The only time there is an exception to this is if after handing over your card, you get sidetracked with another conversation and the person may have forgotten that they didn't get your card yet. In this case, you may politely ask them if it's okay to give them one of your cards.

Many times when you are talking to fellow networkers, you discover a way that you can help him or her out with something. If you make a promise to send someone information or to invite them to another event, make a note of it on their card and be sure you follow through with your promise. They will see that you are dependable and that you do what you say you will do. When it comes to follow up, your word is directly related to your reputation and success. Don't fail to take care of your promises.

"Most of the successful people I've known are the ones who do more listening than talking. "

~ *Bernard M. Baruch*

16

Don't "Throw Up"
on People!

Remember I said, "Don't be the only one talking." Networking veterans refer to this sort of unending monologue as "throwing up all over people" or "verbal diarrhea". Both ideas have very negative connotations and mean that you shouldn't be too eager to share everything that you know, everything you do or everything you have experienced upon the first meeting. There is such a thing as too much information. I promise you, people don't want to know all of that right away. There will be time in the future to talk about your business if you approach the initial meeting correctly. It's much better to get people to share more about themselves. They will leave with the feeling that they've connected very well with you. We have two ears and one mouth for a reason. Try to listen twice as much as you talk.

Search for a connection. See if you know some of the same people or networking groups. Perhaps you work in complimentary fields. For instance, let's say you are a Realtor and they are a mortgage professional or own a home inspection company. Can you do something for this person? Is there a networking group that they may be interested to know about? Can you make a referral or introduction to them that would help them? Make sure you are sincere when you make referrals. Don't just throw names around trying to sound like you know everyone. Again, don't make promises that you know you won't keep. A good networker looks for ways to give first. It will set you apart from the rest in a positive way because far too many people are out there "verbally throwing up" and miss the opportunity to make a positive contribution to other people's businesses.

"Be the one to stand
out in the crowd."

~ *Joel Osteen*

17

Visibility is Better Than Exposure

In a crowd of people, it's important to be visible. Being visible is to be seen clearly with no obstructions. Being exposed conjures up more negative images and alludes to one being a fraud or imposter. There are several ways to be visible and stand out when networking that won't leave you feeling like you've been exposed. If you are authentic and genuine, you never have to be concerned about being exposed or associated with all of the negative implications that word conjures up.

Once you start networking and go from meeting dozens of people to meeting hundreds of people, you may wonder how you can possibly stand out. In a sea of networkers how will you get the attention of everyone in the room? How will they remember you as opposed to the person sitting next to you? You could walk in the room literally naked and you would certainly be noticed and remembered but I don't advise that you go to that extreme. There are many things you can do to get noticed and remembered in positive ways that don't require drastic measures. There are also many mistakes you can make and ways to be remembered in a less than positive light so beware. Choose wisely!

One way to create visibility is to volunteer to speak at some of your networking groups. Many groups welcome speakers for their regular meetings. I know that public speaking may be one of your biggest fears and it is for many people. It was for me, too. Many worry about being judged but remember that people are going to make judgments about you anyway. If you are in control and can create positive visibility then they will have a positive impression even if they haven't met you yet.

Even if the idea of standing up in front of people scares you senseless, try to be open to the idea of speaking. It can accomplish what you are after in a much shorter period of time by allowing roomfuls of people to get to know you all at once without you having to compete for their attention.

After you've been networking for a while, your confidence will undoubtedly grow and you will have had many opportunities to hear other speakers. You can learn a little from each one you hear even if it's what not to do. Speaking is a natural progression from networking once you've gained some confidence. If you had told me when I first started that in a few short years I would become a professional speaker, consultant and teach thousands of people, I would have laughed! But that is just how fast things can change.

Keep in mind when you get the opportunity to speak in front of a group that people really don't want to hear you stand up and drone on and on about your business, especially if it's something really technical. Most people won't be able to follow you and will tune you out. They want to know about you! Tell them how you got started, why you got into your business, what experiences have you had that were funny or memorable. Tell them about your hobbies or where you came from. Just make it personal and give people the opportunity to relate to you and get to know you better.

Remember what I said about industry jargon. You've only got a few seconds to capture their attention. They want to know about you and how you may be able to help them, not about the technicalities of your business. Don't be afraid to share your journey and your hobbies. Each time you speak, you will improve, gain confidence and it will become easier! The bonus is that it's a great way to get in front a larger audience and leverage your time. Wouldn't it be much better to stand in a room of 100 people and speak than to go to an event where you only meet three or four people? If you are the speaker, everyone will have the chance to connect with and remember you! Being a speaker not only leverages your time very effectively, it also is a great way to build your expert status.

There are even networking groups that teach you how to become a speaker. Toastmasters International is one of the largest and most recognized groups that you can join to help prepare you for speaking and there are meetings in most every area. Or you can do an online search for Meetups for speakers.

Just be mindful when you get involved in speaking groups to keep your identity. Usually, you are given assignments each week to write various types of speeches. You will practice doing speeches within the group and be critiqued by the other members. Some of these groups may focus too much on the umms and filler words rather than on the passion and conviction that a speaker brings to the room. Filler words are something that you should most definitely work on eliminating as much as possible, especially if it's preventing your audience from hearing the message, but don't beat yourself up if you throw in a filler word every once in a while. People will remember your message and how you make them feel not how many times you say umm. Again, this is something that you really need to be "naked" with. Being authentic and genuine will go a long way toward helping you connecting with your audience even if your delivery isn't as polished as someone else's right now.

I have a friend that is a member of Toastmasters International and she says that she would never have been comfortable enough to make presentations without the training that she's received due to her involvement in that group. She said that practicing so much within the group has given her the self-confidence needed to get in front of large audiences and speak with poise.

You may even consider hiring a coach or consultant if you feel that you need help with public speaking. One of my networking connections is a successful speaker in my area and I noticed one time on a social media site that she was offering a free 30 minute phone call to the first five people that signed up. I took advantage of the offer and actually learned a great deal of information in those 30 minutes. It was time well spent for me. Anytime a successful speaker is offering advice, pay attention. You never know what you will learn.

There are also seminars and webinars that teach public speaking that can be valuable in getting you started or helping improve your current skills. Dale Carnegie is probably the most widely known. They can offer very valuable assistance especially if you are thinking of speaking as a career move. You can also look for professional speakers that you admire on social media sites and follow them. Many times they post valuable free tips that can help you with your speaking career.

I never thought I would become a professional speaker but it has become part of my brand and it's a natural fit for me. It's a brilliant way to let large groups of people know more about my business, who I am and what I have to offer. I never dreamed when I got chosen to give that ten-minute speech a few years ago that it would lead me to writing this book, becoming a professional speaker and an instructor. Now I'm the one doing the consultations helping others get started on their journey to become a speaker.

Speaking will open many doors and create opportunities for you if you approach it the right way. Think of it like mass networking. You will get in front of a much larger audience than just speaking with individuals one at a time. If you are speaking on a subject pertaining to your profession, you will set yourself apart as an expert in your field. It's the perfect way to market yourself as long as you don't make your speech a sales pitch. Instead, share your story and provide useful information to those that may need your services.

When you are speaking to groups who are affiliated with your profession, it's okay to get a little more detailed and use some of that industry specific language. That's an audience that will understand the jargon. However, if the audience is more diversified then try to keep it more general so people who are not in your profession will be able to get something out of your presentation. Even if they don't completely understand what you do, they will still perceive you as a professional and expert in your field and will be more likely to speak favorably about you to other professionals.

A few tips for you if you're thinking of giving speaking a shot. The most powerful thing you can do when speaking is to motivate and inspire others. Be positive and make your audience feel good. Jump right into your speech. Don't start by thanking the audience. People will immediately tune out if you do that. Make sure you project your voice so even the people in the back of the room can hear you. Make eye contact with people in the front and the back of the room. If you are given 30 minutes to speak, do not go over that time. People get restless. In fact, it's better to end a few minutes early. Have a clear and concise end to your speech. Remember that you are in control of the room. Don't let questions be your downfall. If you must take them, only allow a few and make sure you repeat the question for the audience who may not have been able to hear it. Don't end with questions. Give a brief wrap up after the Q & A. I prefer to just tell the audience that I'll be around after the event if they want to talk with me or have any questions. And finally, one very important tip for you if you want to give speaking a try: Be aware of your habits! Watch yourself in the mirror or video yourself and look at what you do with your hands, body and face when you are speaking. If you have distracting habits, then work diligently on changing those.

I was recently giving one of my three-hour continuing education classes for Realtors and at the first break my colleague, who had accompanied me, came up and whispered for me to put the water bottle down. I was a little confused as to why he was telling me this. It was a three-hour class. I needed water. He went on to tell me that I had apparently been stroking the water bottle in a very distracting manner. Yikes! He said if he noticed it, everybody in the room noticed it.

When I thought about it, I realized that he was right. I did have a habit of running the bottle through my fingers when I was holding on to it. I can promise you, I'll be aware of that little habit for the rest of my life! I'll never hold onto the water bottle while I'm speaking again. I don't want to be noticed and remembered that way! Again, be aware of what you are doing with your hands when you are in front of a room.

Another way to get noticed is to bring a quality door prize to networking events. Many groups will also give you extra time to talk in front of the group if you bring a door prize. Some networking events will even list door prize donors on the invitations and event pages. It's just another way to get noticed and be remembered in a good light. Let's be very clear about this though. When I say door prize, I don't mean a pen or a koozie or other 'freebie'! Those are okay for give-a-ways but it's not a doorprize. Remember, I said quality!

A door prize needs to be something concrete that the recipient can claim. A discount for services is not a door prize. It's a coupon. A 30-minute consultation so you can try to sell your stuff to someone is not a door prize. That's a selling opportunity for you. Anything that requires the winner to spend money isn't a real prize! Invest in something that will be memorable for all the right reasons. Think about the kinds of things that you would personally get excited about winning. Don't waste your money on cheap boring stuff. That'll get you noticed for the wrong reasons. I like to bring a nice bottle of wine with my own custom label. It has my logo and contact information on it. That way, when they are enjoying the wine, they will think of me.

At one of my networking events, someone brought champagne glasses from Tiffany & Co. They were nicely boxed and packaged in the signature Tiffany blue bag. Everyone that approached the table with all of door prizes asked who had donated the Tiffany gift. Don't you think that person knew exactly how they were representing themselves? The person that brought that prize got noticed and talked about by almost everyone there. That door prize made a classy statement and I still talk about it in almost every class I teach!

Since we are talking about door prizes, let's discuss a problem that I've witnessed too many times. Typically, you are asked to drop your card in a bowl to enter to win a door prize. I beg you, please, please do not try to stack the deck on winning by putting in more than one card! Also, don't attempt to bend your card so it will stick out. This is childish and silly and it doesn't work. When the host is going through the cards after the event, they will most certainly notice what you have done and they will make judgments about you. They will probably also share that judgment with others and you will immediately get branded a cheater or as desperate. I promise those door prizes are not worth your dignity or reputation.

Another issue, don't try to steal the door prizes. What?! Yes, I have witnessed this. I actually watched a woman load up her purse with $10 Starbucks gift cards that were to be given away as door prizes. She lost all of her integrity with me for a few cups of coffee! Your integrity should be worth a lot more than that. So please, resist the temptation to pilfer the loot! People are always watching!

If you don't win something, be happy for the person who did win. I've seen way too many vultures when it comes to drawings for door prizes. If a person happens to be in the restroom when their card is drawn, don't plead and argue for another card to be drawn. Help track down the winner instead! I realize much of this sounds completely juvenile and it is! Yet I've seen grown adults, and otherwise respected business people, behave in this way, which is why I'm pointing it out. I've seen people do these things repeatedly and for what? To say they won something once? These kinds of stories linger and don't think that just because you are in a large city, that the stories don't follow you. They do.

Sometimes you will see a community table where you can display promo materials for your business. This is a good way to get noticed too. Be sure to take advantage of this opportunity but don't abuse it. Never put your flyers or cards on top of someone else's or even worse, remove a competitor's promo packets. Again, people are watching your every move. Make sure you pick up the leftover material at the end of the event. Don't make the host have to try to get it back to you or even worse, throw it away. You spent money on those materials. Don't waste them.

If there isn't a community table set up to display brochures, don't presume that you can place your promo materials on the host check-in table. When I've hosted events I've had people put stacks of their stuff down right in front of me on the check in table. Sorry folks, that space is reserved for the person that put the event together. Respect the space. I actually had a lady put her magazine in front of my sign at an event that I was hosting. It was incredibly presumptuous. Is that the way you want to be remembered?

Also, never set up your wares like a door-to-door vacuum salesman! If there isn't a preset spot to display your wares, do not show up with boxes of your materials expecting to set up shop! I hosted an event one time that was in a very high end swanky bar. A lady showed up with her cardboard box full of wares that she wanted to showcase on top of this tacky used cardboard box. Needless to say, we had to have a word about it. It was awkward for everyone. Don't be the one that the host remembers for this kind of behavior.

You can volunteer to help the host at conferences, seminars and networking events to increase your visibility. For instance, they may need help with checking people in. Think about it; if you are sitting at the check-in desk you can meet virtually everyone that walks in the door and immediately put faces with names. This will give you a huge advantage in meeting the people you want to connect with very quickly. You'll also get a chance to meet the organizers and speakers before things get busy and they get bombarded with people. Who knows, it may even provide you with an opportunity to get on the speaker's list for the next event. It's a perfect way to stand out and the host will appreciate the help!

Remember to take photos at events and post them on Social Media. People love to see themselves in photos and when you post them, you'll connect with everyone in the photos. Make sure you also take advantage of photo opportunities as well. Jump in with a smile! Getting seen at networking events lets people know that you aren't afraid to get out there and make new connections. You'll look like a mover and shaker in the networking scene.

Sponsoring an event is also great way to get noticed and stand out. It doesn't have to cost a lot of money. In fact, you shouldn't think of it as a cost. It's an investment in your business. A sponsor can offer to purchase appetizers, flowers, door prizes, or print materials or many of the other things that may be provided at an event. Many times, sponsors are recognized during the event or on promotional materials so it puts your name in front of all the invited guests. It will get you noticed by people that may not even attend the event. Even if only 100 people show up to an event, it's likely that 1000 were invited. If you are one of the sponsors, all of those people who were invited saw your name on the invitations. When you are consistent with this kind of promotion, people start remembering your name. You will stand out.

One of the best ways to stand out is to host your own event. I've hosted quite a few happy hour types of events and can speak from personal experience when I say that it is tremendously effective. Hosting just requires a little time to find a venue and send invitations. You don't have to make it complicated. I have a basic formula when I'm searching for the right venue for a happy hour networking event. If you can find a place that looks and feels professional, is free to use, has easy accessibility, easy parking, and has food and drinks available then you have found yourself a great spot! Keep looking until you've checked off all of these things.

Make sure you choose a spot that has a professional vibe. Restaurants, bars and clubs are fine but stay away from fast food type establishments or places that cater to a super young crowd or have questionable reputations.

You don't need to pay for a room to have your party. Some places will want to charge you but there are plenty of places that will give you a room for free and are happy to do so with the understanding that your guests will be purchasing food and/or drinks. If an establishment wants to charge you for the space, I suggest that you move on and consider another spot. Restaurants and bars are great places to start. Hotels generally charge you for their rooms but there are some that will allow you to come in for free. Once you've established a reputation for successful events, you will have great referrals for future venues.

Accessibility is vital. You want to find a venue that is in the area where your guests will be. Most networkers won't want to drive across town to attend an event. Parking also needs to be easy. It's ideal if valet parking is an option but not mandatory. Some people refuse to use valet service. They don't let other people drive their car. Others may really want valet service available. If it's bad weather, valet service can be invaluable. Nobody wants to walk through the rain, snow or a windstorm to get to a meeting and risk entering the venue looking like a drowned cat! We also don't want to hike from a parking garage in high heels and men don't like to trudge through puddles in sharply shined shoes.

There should be drinks and appetizers available for purchase. Whether it's a breakfast, lunch, or happy hour event, people will want food available. A lot of people who are nervous feel comforted just by holding something in their hand even if it is as simple as a cookie and glass of ice water. Bringing in a food sponsor for appetizers is an ideal scenario for someone with a limited budget. At a happy hour type of event people will appreciate light bites as they have most likely come to the event from work and will not have had anything to eat since lunch. Cost for finger foods won't be as high as sponsoring a full meal. Another type of sponsor you may want to consider is a drink sponsor. They could purchase the first drink for guests.

As mentioned above, door prizes keep things exciting. I like to have five or six items to give away. I caution you not to allow cheap door prizes or to have too many. If you have a large number of them, giving them away can become management intensive and take too much time to deal with during the event. You want to be able to mingle with the guests and if you are tied up the whole time giving away door prizes then you've defeated the purpose of hosting an event.

You should also be aware that people might show up with something to donate that you didn't anticipate. I've had this happen at nearly every event I've hosted despite my pleas and instructions to speak to me first if someone has a door prize they'd like to donate. You will have to decide how you want to deal with this. I once had a lady show up with homemade hair ties made from old t-shirts. They were a cute idea but they certainly didn't belong on the table next to the Tiffany champagne glasses.

Sometimes you will flat out have to decline offers and this can get tricky. People get their feelings hurt so you'll have to navigate this with a little diplomacy. I give people guidelines on the expected value of door prizes when they ask me about donations. This way I set proper expectations before we even start talking about what they have in mind to donate. When the lady showed up with the hair ties I thanked her first then told her that they were cute and I appreciated her thoughtfulness but they weren't right for that type of event. I also added that I'd keep them in mind if I ever hosted an event where I thought they'd be the right fit.

In my opinion, Tuesdays, Wednesdays and Thursdays are the best nights to host Happy Hour events. Mondays tend to be hectic stress filled days for many people and they may not get away from work early enough to make it to an event in the early evening. Fridays are either family night or date night for many people plus they are tired of talking shop by the end of the week. After about noon on Friday they slowly check out of work mode and start going into weekend mode. Check the calendar for obvious conflicts like holidays or major sporting events. There will always be many things going on so don't be concerned if you want to have an event on a night that another group regularly meets.

Don't worry if your first event doesn't draw 100 people. As long as you don't lure people there and then expect them to sit through a long or boring presentation, your reputation as a host will grow and so will the attendance. They'll want to come again if they enjoyed it and made some good connections. You will eventually develop a reputation for being a great host and before you know it, you will need larger spaces to accommodate the crowds that gather when you host an event. Just be nice, treat people right and get out there and do something!

If you want to host a regularly occurring breakfast or lunch type of event the formula is still basically the same as for happy hour events with just a little more structure. Find a venue, decide what kind of format you want to follow and start inviting people. Many restaurants have small rooms available for meetings like this and are happy to give you the space if people are ordering food and drinks. I like to keep things really simple and have no desire to manage things that don't need to be managed. For that reason, I don't recommend charging fees to attend. Just let people come in and pay for what they order.

A few things to remember when taking charge of a group: make sure that you pay attention to, and enforce, start and end times. Don't let people take advantage of their allotted time to speak, allow time for actual networking, and just be normal and don't get gimmicky or weird! One group I know of puts a rubber bracelet on you and insists that you wear it until you have brought in three people that join the group. That could take a while. Most people don't like that pushy mentality. A few rules and a little structure is necessary for a good flow to your meetings but it's important to allow people to network in their own comfort zone.

Growth of a group is important but some people are never going to be comfortable in the role of a recruiter so don't make too many requirements of your members. The fewer rules the better. If you follow these basic guidelines, you will continue to have good, productive people show up for your events and the growth will be a natural occurrence. You won't have to bully others into bringing in everyone they meet off the streets to satisfy silly quotas.

These are all great ways to stand out and get noticed among the hundreds of networkers in your area. Go ahead and give some of these things a try and you'll see that you will make great new connections from stepping up and standing out.

"You gotta know when to hold 'em, know when to fold 'em, know when to walk away, know when to run."

~ *Kenny Rogers*

18

Don't Be Afraid to Walk Away!

Learn when it's time to move on. Remember, networking is a little like speed dating. Be prepared to have a lot of five-minute conversations. You aren't going to like everybody and they aren't all going to like you. It's okay!

I have encountered a few oddballs out there in the networking world and there is an art to removing yourself from strange or uncomfortable situations. I've had to learn these techniques through real life experiences. I vividly remember one event that I attended. It was the launch of a new group so I had no idea what to expect but I decided to go give it a try. As I entered the venue, a man with a strangely lopsided toupee approached me and proudly said, "You must be a zero!" I had no idea where he was going with this. In my mind, I was wondering if this was one of those events where they have icebreakers in the form of games where you must gather information about the other guests.

My business partner was much quicker on her feet than I was and let out a big sigh and proceeded to turn on her heel and walk away. I just stood there and said, "huh?" As he uttered his next statement, it all became clear to me. He told me that he used to be really thin too and now that he has a desk job and has gained a lot of weight, and as he yammered on and on, I zoned out. He had been referring to my clothing size! Obviously this is not a normal or appropriate networking conversation topic. I was still fairly new to networking and had no idea how to politely exit this inappropriate conversation. Fortunately for me, my business partner returned and rescued me from this bizarre exchange. We circulated around the room and found some networkers who were eager to have more conventional types of conversations.

I have since learned that it's perfectly fine to politely excuse yourself from a ridiculous conversation and move on. There's no need to be rude but you can say; "Excuse me, I need to go speak to someone over there." Don't waste your time with people who are clearly inappropriate, but don't get completely upset by it either, just move on. If you can, go with a friend who can help you out with situations like this. And by all means, don't be the person engaging in this kind of inappropriate banter. It may seem harmless at the time, but it is not and it will get you a bad reputation quickly.

Another time, I decided to try out a women's group that had been sending me invitations relentlessly. I tried to do my homework first but I couldn't really get any concrete information so I had no idea what to expect. I should have seen the warning signs when no one could answer my questions before the event. I decided to give it a try anyway. After about 30 minutes of mingling, we were asked to take a seat so the program could get started. I felt a little uneasy about some of the things that were being said by the people that I'd met so I found a seat near the door. After a short time, it became clear that this was a politically slanted women's movement that I didn't want to be a part of or associated with in any way. I quietly made an exit. There is no need to make a spectacle of leaving if you don't agree with what is going on. Just get up like you are heading to the restroom and leave. Don't feel compelled to stay and waste your time, but also don't make a point to irritate or upset anyone else. Just make sure you have your escape route planned in case it's the wrong place for you! This is also a lesson in trusting your instincts. I picked up a strange vibe very quickly which turned out to be right. If you don't feel comfortable or get the idea that something is not right, trust that feeling and be on your way. There will be other events.

Above all, be safe. Networking is all about meeting new people and sharing what you do so it's necessary to start conversations with many strangers. I warn you though, to be very careful about what information you provide to complete strangers. Unfortunately, there are people out there that will use networking groups as a way to find potential targets for scams, stalking or other types of nefarious activity. Don't provide too much personal information. If your instincts are telling you to walk away from a conversation, then by all means, walk away! In this case, don't worry about being rude if you are truly worried about your own personal safety.

When I was a newbie, I eagerly shared all kinds of personal information with people who asked me questions. I had to learn the hard way that you must listen to your instincts. I met a man who founded and ran a well-known national business. During the course of our conversation, he asked me a few personal questions such as what city I lived in. By answering these seemingly innocent questions, he did a small amount of research and actually found exactly where I lived. The next time I saw him he let it be known that he had driven to my house. He had found out all kinds of personal information about me and other family members.

Yes, I got cold chills when I learned this. He would show up at networking events and come up behind me and whisper things in my ear. This wasn't a case of a man with a serious crush. He crossed the line by searching for my house. He called and stalked me for about a year before he presumably moved on to another unwitting victim. It could have been much worse than it was, but what happened to me was enough to open my eyes when it comes to sharing too much. Be safe and always trust your instincts!

"The impression you make on people through your handshake influences how they feel about you."

~ *Todd Smith*

19

Handshakes and Bear Hugs!

I'm sure you have heard the phrase, "When in Rome, do as the Romans." Where networking is concerned, this means you want to fit into the business world but it doesn't mean that you need to disregard your own culture and beliefs. It just means to be respectful of the country that you are in and the people that you meet. If you are in America and you aren't familiar with American business etiquette then you must make an effort to learn it. It's up to you to educate yourself. Buy a book, search online or hire an etiquette coach if you need help.

This is especially true when greeting other professionals. The first impression you give someone is extremely important. Having said this, Americans should also be respectful of other cultures as well. You will encounter people with all types of backgrounds and beliefs. There will be people from many diverse cultures with different styles of greetings. Remember, manners are really about respecting others and not making people feel uncomfortable or awkward.

The way you greet someone leaves a lasting impression so make sure it's appropriate and professional. Even your method of shaking hands sends many messages about you and your confidence. Handshaking etiquette in business is different than in social settings and different cultures observe different rules. I am going to give you a short lesson on how you should greet a fellow business person in an American business environment.

In my classes and training seminars, I'm shocked by how many people ask me about the correct way to greet other business professionals. Hopefully I can clear things up a bit. Here are the basics of business handshakes: If you are a large person with a very strong grip, be aware of that grip especially if the other person is small or wearing rings. Ouch! While this can happen with anyone, I've seen it most often when very strong men shake hands with a woman. Even when it's two men shaking hands, it's not meant to be a he-man show of strength and testosterone. Don't pump her/his hand so vigorously that you knock that person off balance. Develop a self-adjusting handshake based on whom you are greeting.

If you are sitting down and someone approaches you and extends a hand, then stand up to shake hands. While you don't want to give an overly strong handshake, please don't offer the limp and lifeless "fish hand". Offer a firm hand. Remember you are in a business setting. If you offer a limp hand you are sending a message that you lack confidence. Worse than the "fish hand" is the delicate finger and thumb handshake. This may be appropriate for the cotillion but this is business. Shake hands like you mean it! Extend your entire hand, thumbs up, all the way to where the webbing of your thumbs touch. Shake from the elbow, not the shoulder. Once you have engaged in a handshake, keep it short. Your handshake should last only a few seconds. No lingering, holding or excessive pumping is necessary. Don't grab your connected hands with your left hand and form a trap, or grip their upper arm. That's a much more intimate greeting and not appropriate in business settings with people you don't know. The double grip is known as the politician's handshake for a reason. It doesn't seem genuine, especially if you are meeting someone for the first time.

There seems to be a great deal of confusion when it comes to women and shaking hands. I think this stems from some of the older etiquette advice that seems to persist even in the business world. Many years ago, a woman didn't shake hands at all. But I'd like to point out that most women didn't own businesses either, or at least not the kind of businesses where they needed to meet other business owners. Now women in the boardroom are a common occurrence so it's way past time to move on from that way of thinking. Today, women in the business world shake hands just as men do. I urge women to take the initiative here and extend your hand first. Some men are unsure of what to do because of all of the old-fashioned rules they've heard or have floating around in their heads. Do them a favor and set them at ease by showing them it is okay to shake hands.

I almost hate to bring this up, but the issue of sexual harassment has gotten so much notice that many men would not even touch a woman in a business setting. You can't blame them really, as no one

173

wants to be accused of something. If you are a woman, then make the first move and put other business owners at ease with an upfront and professional handshake.

Before you even think about extending your hand, there is something that you must keep in mind. Make sure that you make eye contact. There is no bigger error than shaking a person's hand while carrying on a conversation with someone else. Don't extend a hand if you can't look the person in the eye and speak directly to them. It's beyond rude to shake hands and never even look at the individual you are supposed to be greeting. The opposite of this, but an equally offensive approach, is to thrust your hand upon someone in mid-conversation with someone else. You are interrupting them and this is not appreciated. Pay attention to what is going on around you!

Occasionally, I get questions about the fist bump that seems to have gained popularity among Generation Y young professionals and in casual settings. I personally don't think it's a good choice in professional networking environments. It's too familiar and relaxed for a first time business greeting. You should stick to the handshake upon meeting other business professionals.

If you are greeting a friend or long time business associate at a business function, I cautiously advise you to greet them as you normally would whether it is a fist bump, hug, air kiss, hand holding shake, or double cheek kiss. If your normal greeting includes something more intimate, then perhaps you should tone it down a bit for business occasions. I'll add a word of caution here; in business settings, please don't squeeze anyone in a bear hug so tight that you can feel their rib cage and their face turns blue from lack of air. For that matter, don't do that ever! If you are not in an intimate relationship, it is completely inappropriate to embrace with all of your full frontal bits connecting. You don't need to get that familiar with anyone in public. If you are in an intimate relationship with someone at a networking event, then save the full body hug for a more private environment.

If you want an effective way to ward off those super friendly people known for that awkward bear hug embrace, move in on his/her side. Stand beside the person, put your arm around their back, and lean over so you can give him/her a side hug. If he/she tries to swing around to give you the full frontal hug, use your hand on the opposite side to give that person a firm pat on the shoulder. He/she should get your message. This way no feelings are hurt and you won't have to deal with squeezing yourself out of the full body embrace. Awkwardness averted!

I am reminded of a story when I was still fairly new to networking. I approached a group of four people sitting at a table and introduced myself to them. One of them was just finishing up with a plate of appetizers and was engrossed in picking the food from her teeth with her fingernail. Needless to say that was inappropriate. Introductions were made, hands were extended and we proceeded to shake hands. When it came around to this particular woman, she sucked the recently extracted food from her fingernail and eagerly extended her hand for a handshake. Not knowing how to handle this, and holding back a gag, I reluctantly obliged her. Shortly after that, I excused myself to the ladies room and thoroughly washed my hands. I was completely grossed out by shaking her wet fingers and will forever remember this particular woman for this behavior. Even though she's a sweet lady, I still don't like to shake her hand. Don't be that person.

Today, I would handle this situation much differently. First of all, I wouldn't even allow the whole hand-shaking thing to get started if I see that even one person in a group is eating. It inevitably leads to the nasty scene I just described (or one similar to it) and germs being spread. If it looks like someone may be inclined to offer a wet finger (covered with saliva or salad dressing or wing sauce or whatever!), I try to head them off at the pass by stating that I can see they are eating and suggest that we save the handshake for later for their hygienic purposes.

Many times when I'm teaching my networking class, I get questions about reasons to avoid handshaking and how to handle it if you don't shake hands. One very petite lady in particular said she had arthritis and that shaking hands was very painful for her. Other people have raised objections based on germ related issues, especially during flu season. This is a very tricky situation and should be approached delicately. Some of the options you have are to keep your hands behind your back and slightly bow upon greeting someone. Or you could hold something in your hands, which sends a signal that you aren't open to hand shaking. Still, people will notice your reluctance and wonder why you aren't shaking hands. This will even cause some people to feel insulted. I suggest good old-fashioned honesty and just say that you don't shake hands because of arthritis, flu season, religious reasons or whatever the cause may be. Some people may still be offended but there isn't much you can do about every single person's feelings. Just be kind about it and most reasonable people will respect your view.

Another common question is in regard to the issue of who should offer their hand first in the handshake. While this book specifically addresses networking scenarios, I'll also cover a couple of other areas that seem to have people confused where handshakes are concerned. If you are greeting someone of higher stature, such as your boss or someone who is interviewing you, then you should allow a second for him or her to extend a hand first. This is proper etiquette. I caution you to not wait too long if they don't offer a hand. It will become awkward and perhaps they aren't aware of this expectation. This is just an FYI for you to keep in the back of your mind but don't use it to miss an opportunity to extend your hand and make a positive impression.

The other issue I hear about is whose hand gets to be on top but the answer is: neither! Both people's hands should face each other with thumbs on the top. There really shouldn't be any leveraging for position during a handshake. Please don't take cues from politicians and start twisting your fellow networkers' wrists so your hand can be on top. Handshaking is not a sporting event. You don't win anything that way, I promise!

"Every survival kit
should include a
sense of humor."

~ Author Unknown

20

Bring Your Sense of Humor

You will most definitely meet some eccentric types of people out there, just as you do in any life situation. The trick is to be able to roll with it and keep smiling. I have learned that networking requires a great sense of humor. Yes, you must follow your instincts but you don't have to be paranoid either. If you can't enter a room with a sense of humor and a smile, then consider skipping the networking event. If you've had a dreadful day or you are just in a sour mood, stay at home. You won't do yourself any good by trying to meet new people if you are in a negative place or a bad mood. If you decide to go anyway, you'll undoubtedly see someone that you'll want to share your terrible day with. Your arms will begin flailing as you relay the events of the day that have you upset. People will read your body language and sense the negativity going on. Needless to say, it doesn't make a great first impression.

I have been invited to all kinds of crazy networking events. I have had a woman extend to me a bowl of popcorn that was held in the same hand where she was holding her shoes. Apparently her feet hurt.

I later heard her remark that she couldn't believe that no one there liked popcorn! I have been tricked into watching long presentations, and into attending politically slanted movements. Suffice it to say, that I have just about seen it all. That's why I'm sharing all of these experiences with you. You'll be better prepared than I was to smile and keep going until you find the right networking groups where you can make beneficial, professional business connections.

There are many more great events than there are strange ones and I've made fantastic connections by not giving up just because some events, or people, leave you walking away shaking your head in wonder. Most will have you walking away with a pocket full of cards from motivated professionals just like yourself. Every single sponsor that I have ever gotten on my website, WomansInSite.com, has come from networking! Every speaking engagement and consulting session has come from some type of networking connection!

All networking events have unique personalities and atmospheres. You will find some that you like and others that you will want to run from as fast as possible. Be sure to ask questions if it's a group that you are not familiar with. Find out how the meetings are structured. Ask if there are speakers and if visitors are encouraged to participate or just allowed to observe. I attended some real doozies before I learned to ask questions about each new group before I went. At least I have some entertaining stories to share from these crazy events!

One of the most memorable networking events that I attended was a woman's group. It was held in the open courtyard of an old home that was converted into a rustic type of event venue. My former business partner and I thought we'd stop by and check it out on our way to another event that we were going to. I'd been invited several times to visit this group and just wanted to see what it was all about. When we arrived, we were led outside to a large courtyard area where the other ladies were all sitting in chairs in a circle. I quickly got the feeling that this was going to be a little different so I made a point to say that we had another event to go to and couldn't stay very long. We were shown chairs and invited to sit down and join the conversation. My first thought was how dirty the chairs were. It looked like they hadn't been wiped down in about 30 years and they were full of leaves and sticks from the huge trees overhead. I felt like I was on a weird camping trip and forgot to bring my jeans and marshmallows for roasting. I tilted the chair so at least the loose debris would fall out and I reluctantly sat down. I couldn't help but wonder how dirty my pants would be when I stood up. Looking back, I should have declined the offer to sit down and join them. It got a little wacky!

The leader of the group talked for a while and we all introduced ourselves and said a little about our businesses. I noticed that most of the people there were in some quirky types of new age businesses. It was definitely a group of free spirits!

As things were wrapping up, we were all asked to "put out to the universe" what we were looking for and ask for affirmation from the group. Then each person in the group was to give an affirmation of acceptance to the speaker. I remember trying to quickly think of a way to opt out of this peculiar ritual without insulting the ladies who were obviously quite serious about it. You know how it is when laughter is totally inappropriate but it's bubbling up inside of you ready to explode! My friend and I were avoiding eye contact because I knew we'd burst into uncontrollable laughter if we even looked at each other. As it went around the circle, her turn came before mine and she totally shocked me by playing along and making an impressive acting debut. She wholeheartedly threw herself into the role and put her dream out to the universe and made a huge show by opening her arms wide asking for affirmation and acceptance. I could have died! It was all I could do to keep my composure and not burst out laughing. I don't even remember what I said, but somehow managed to get through it. We got out of there as quickly as possible after that. As soon as the car doors closed we both laughed so hard that tears were streaming down our faces. I'm sure there are people that fit in that type of group but we were clearly not those people!

Another amusing networking group I visited was a group of women who wanted to teach women how to talk to men to be able to negotiate effectively and succeed. After the meeting started they went into a role-playing exercise and, as luck would have it, I was chosen to be a participant. The leaders actually got annoyed with me because I wouldn't really get mad at the pretend man that I was supposed to be role playing with. They kept trying to steer the interaction to one of anger. We went round and round with their dialogue and I didn't budge. Their motivation was to get me angry so they could show me a better way to deal with men. They wanted to show me how to flirt! For the record, I think we all learn that in preschool and it is completely inappropriate in a business setting.

I just wasn't feeling it, nor did I agree with the premise that this was even a valid approach for a professional group. Instead, I was becoming increasingly annoyed at their supposition that if you flirt with a man, you can get whatever you want out of him. Not only in personal relationships, but they were actually recommending that as a way of doing business with men which I utterly disagree with. What made this group even more laughable is that they tried to sell me coaching to help me strengthen my relationships with men. Ironically enough, none of these women were actually in relationships! They represented themselves as a networking group but clearly function as a 'land a man' group. You can't make this stuff up! Again, ask questions of the group leader and if you know someone who has attended a previous event, try to get a feel for the focus and goal of the group. It will save you a lot of time and energy.

Even though I've experienced some strange people and events, I still keep getting out there and trying new events. Why, because I keep my sense of humor. I don't let the crazies of this world keep me from trusting that there is more out there for me. Be open to trying new groups. Just think, it may give you a funny story of our own to share with others and have some laughs about down the road. I have learned to do a little homework in advance and ask more questions but sometimes you just have to take a chance and go for it. If you can speak to the host or an active member of a group before you go, ask about the philosophy, emphasis and structure of the group. Inquire about joining fees and rules. If it sounds like it's not something that you'd be into then keep searching for one that fits your style. There are many great networking groups out there so don't get discouraged if you occasionally run across one that tests your sense of humor. When you find a good one, go and keep going consistently!

SECTION 4

You've Shown Up Naked All Over Town

"You are what you do, not what you say you'll do."

~ C.G. Jung

21

Now What?

Do you have a pile of business cards on your desk? Now that you have gotten out and met tons of new people, what do you do with all of those great connections? Your next step is the one that many people miss so don't be that person and you'll be a step ahead of most networkers. This part is extremely important!

You can have your brand in place, impressive business cards, a professional wardrobe, an irresistible introduction that wows, impeccable manners and regularly attend all the best events but none of it matters if you skip the follow through. You must make use of the connections that you have made. Whether you are a personal trainer, financial advisor, hairdresser, or engineer it is essential that you have a way to continue the conversations that you have started. It doesn't matter what profession you are in, the steps are all the same.

One of the most important items of business is if you have made promises to send people information about other events, to connect them with someone in your networking circle, or follow up in some way, then make sure you actually do it in a reasonable amount of time! I recommend making some kind of connection within 24 hours if at all possible. Send them the information for that event you promised to send or make the introduction that you led them to believe that you could make. Make your word mean something! Follow through with what you say you will do. Many people fail to do this, or fail to do it in a timely manner, so by taking action, you'll stand out and make a great impression.

Networking: Naked & Unafraid • Kathryn Crawford Wheat

---✺---

"Find someone new
to meet and help.
Have ZERO agenda
on how this helps
you. Just make them
better in some way.
Seek nothing
in return."

~ Chris Brogan

---✺---

22

What to Do With All Those Cards

Once you get back to your office, make three stacks from the business cards you collected at the event. One stack is for the people that you want to meet with for a one-on-one. If you network a lot, you know that you don't actually have time to sit down with each person you have met and have a one-hour meeting. You do actually have to work some, right? I urge you to be selective when deciding whom you want to immediately schedule time with. These should be the people that you feel you have an immediate and obvious business connection with. They are the ones that you know can be an asset in your business or would be a valuable referral if the relationship works out. Again, don't be too quick to form a partnership. Get to know them a little first. Learn about how they do business and if that is a good fit for what you do. Sometimes what seems like a great fit really isn't so this time is necessary to uncover those issues. If it is a great fit, then you can proceed and explore ways to work together.

The second stack is for people that you want to stay in touch with but don't have an immediate need to get together and consider doing business with. The relationship may develop into one where you decide to have a one-on-one later but you are just keeping in touch for now. These people may be supporters of you or simply enjoy hearing from you from time to time. The idea is to just keep the conversation going.

Don't think that you have to allow the second stack of cards to gather dust on your desk. When you initially meet people and get their card, ask them if it's okay to add them to your email list. Most people will tell you yes and you can make that notation on the back of their business card. If they say no, then don't take it personally. It just means that they're not your person. They're not that into you and that is okay! For the people that I do want to stay in touch with, I send them a very short email within a couple of days after our initial meeting. I tell them that I enjoyed meeting them and that I'd like to stay in touch. I'm letting them know for a second time that I'll be sending them emails. If there is something in particular that I remember about my conversation with them, I may make reference to that in the email as well. This makes it more personal. The most important thing is that I don't try to sell them anything. Then I add them to my email list where they will hear from me every week or two.

Other options for that second stack of cards are to send a personal note or card. Few people actually take the time to send a handwritten note so if you do this then you will certainly stand out in a positive way. I have a friend that keeps a box of "Thank You" notes in her car along with envelopes, stamps and a pen. That way when she leaves a meeting, she immediately writes the note and gets it ready to go. This takes some discipline but is a wonderful idea.

If sending a handwritten note is something that you don't realistically see yourself actually doing, then another great choice is

Send Out Cards. It's like a bridge between high tech and a personal touch. They make sending cards super easy! Send Out Cards allows you to send personalized custom greeting cards and include photos or even send gifts all from your computer. They even stamp and address the envelope for you. It's another excellent way to maintain business relationships. I'll still put them on my email list so we can stay in touch long term, which I'll explain in detail in a later chapter, but this is a superb way to be remembered among all the other networkers out there.

The third stack is for the few people that you know you don't want to stay in touch with. This stack is super easy to file; it can go straight into the trashcan. These are the people that have walked around handing out cards without speaking to you or the people that have "thrown up" information on you. They really aren't worth any extra time on your part. Instead, spend time on the people in the first and second stack that have potential for building a solid relationship.

"Networking
is marketing.
Marketing yourself,
marketing your
uniqueness,
marketing what you
stand for."

~ Christine Comaford-Lynch

23

One-On-One
Time

You may want to get to know some of your new connections a little better by scheduling a one-on-one. In the networking world, this means that you spend about an hour together usually over coffee, or perhaps lunch, learning a little more about each other. Find a mutually agreeable location. Don't expect the other person to come to your office. At this meeting, you can go into a little more depth about your business, see whom you might know in common and learn how you can help each other. When scheduling your meeting, make sure you are clear about what your intentions are. Let them know what you want to meet with them about. If you aren't clear, it may scare off potential business relationships or worse, get you some unwanted suitors. It's best to each take care of your own tab in situations like this. There are times that it may be acceptable to let the other person buy such as when they have openly told you that they just want to pick your brain. In this case, the least they can do is offer to feed you but even if they don't, that is okay.

I've experienced people who like to schedule one-on-one appointments on the spot at networking events and it is fine to do this, but always confirm your appointment the day before you are to meet. Unfortunately, I've found that some of the appointments that are made on the fly don't get put into people's calendar and they forget. Needless to say, it's a huge waste of time driving to an appointment and waiting for someone who never shows up. In fact, it's a good idea to confirm every appointment you make. Many people are fine with doing this by either sending a short email, by text, or making a quick phone call just to make sure the time slot will still work for them. This will save you valuable time in the long run. If you happen to be running late for an appointment, call or text the person you are going to meet and let them know. You never know, maybe pushing back the meeting time will help them wrap up what they are working on and they will appreciate it. The important thing is to communicate in advance.

When it does come time to meet, know that it's not okay to bring your children to a one-on-one meeting – or really any business meeting. While you may think this goes without saying, once again, I wouldn't point it out if it hadn't happened. I had a lady show up to a meeting one time with her two daughters. If she had simply called me and told me that she had her daughters with her and offered to reschedule then I would most likely have said it was no problem or we could have figured something out that worked better. The funny thing was, the girls were plenty old enough to stay at home by themselves. To top it all off, one of them kept taking pictures of me with her phone. She thought she was being sly but I knew exactly what she was doing. The mom completely ignored her but finally her older sister blurted out, "why are you taking pictures of her?" Everything about the way she handled this situation was unprofessional and inappropriate!

Don't think of a one-on-one as an opportunity to present your sales pitch. I've even seen people show up with charts, graphs, sales brochures and even product videos! Approach it as an opportunity to gather information and explore ways in which you can connect and help each other. Don't go into it expecting to sell the other person on your business. And please, don't try the old bait and switch! Never lure someone to a one-on-one telling them you want to do business with them and expect them to sit through your video presentation. Instead, use this time as a way to get to know each other. It doesn't have to be all business but please stay professional and respectful.

Understand that some people will ask for a one-on-one so they can show you their presentation. Be aware! Ask questions when they ask for a meeting. While you may be so interested that you will want to see a video presentation, you still want to know their intentions upfront.

I once agreed to attend a presentation that a "friend" was having for her business. She knew that I wasn't interested in joining her in her MLM (multi-level marketing) endeavor. She had told me that she was going to be leading the meeting and wanted me to hear her speak. I made it clear that I was solely there to show support. Or so I thought.

Once the presentation was over, my companion was asked to excuse himself and allow for me to have a private conversation with my "friend". Once alone, I was cornered by two of the people in this endeavor and pressured to join. I can't express enough how extremely disappointed I was in this "friend" for using this tactic. I certainly don't view her in the same way anymore. I considered it very disrespectful. No one appreciates feeling tricked or singled out and cornered.

One other thing I feel I must address. A one-on-one is absolutely not a date! Don't ask a person that you have just met to follow up with dinner or drinks. This sends an entirely different message than just networking. If you happen to develop an ongoing relationship with a fellow networker, then it may become okay to meet for drinks or dinner but not on the first one-on-one. I can't tell you how presumptuous it is for a man or woman to assume that a person is out looking for love when he/she is really only trying to grow their business. Even if you have a reason to suspect that there are other motivations for his/her presence and their behavior suggests you may be correct, give him/her the benefit of the doubt and don't make it awkward by flirting with them. You won't create genuine business relationships if they are built on the possibility of sex and you will lose the respect of everyone. Always keep it professional or you may be asked to leave the group!

Friendships and personal relationships can develop from networking relationships. Just proceed slowly and with extreme caution. Remember that you will most likely continue to see that person at future events even if the relationship doesn't work out. You don't want to be the person who has hit on, or dated, everybody in the room. Think ahead about all the "what-ifs".

My disclaimer: I did actually develop a lasting relationship with a man that I initially met while networking. We knew each other for several months before we ever met on a business level and we had many mutual friends that encouraged me to meet with him. As it turns out, we had a lot in common and more than a business relationship developed over time. I knew going in to the relationship that it could be awkward if things didn't work out between us. For me, it's worked out just fine but you still need to think about all the "what-ifs" before you make a similar decision.

"The money is
in the list."

~ Ronald Earl Wilsher

24

Email Magic

Meeting someone at a networking event and starting a conversation is just the first step. Email is a great way to establish a better connection and continue your conversation. If you have a good email system, you'll realize that you don't have to pitch to the room when you are networking. It doesn't have to be the last time you will be seen by that room full of people. You can stay in touch with email. Notice I said, "stay in touch". Don't use email to pitch your business! Use it to simply stay present in people's minds. Of course you can talk about your business a little bit but don't push! Trust me, when they want to know more about what you do, they will ask.

I use an email system called Mail Chimp but there are many similar email systems that you can use to handle your email list. One of the most well known is Constant Contact. I prefer Mail Chimp because it's easy to use. I can personalize it by inserting the recipient's name. I can track the open rate, people can subscribe or unsubscribe if they want to and I can see which links have been clicked on. Once you have set up your template, it's quite easy to just edit the body of the email. Most importantly, at the time of this writing, it's free up to 2000 names. I use email to let people know what's new, to send party or networking invitations and to provide motivation or information that might be valuable to them.

It's great if you can come up with a catchy name for your list that reflects your personality. Caution: the word 'database' just makes people want to run, so don't call it that! It sounds boring and clinical. I call my email list the "In List". It's a great fit for what I do. Put some thought to it and come up with something that's right for your business and fits your personality.

After you get a list started, consistently send out short, interesting emails that will add positivity to the recipient's day. Again, don't be pushy with sales or people will stop opening your emails or unsubscribe. Use this as a way to engage people. Let them get to know a little more about you, your hobbies or whatever it is that makes you unique. Keep it short. Provide useful information. Let people know about upcoming events that you want to share. The idea is to keep your name on people's minds. They will remember you if they consistently hear from you.

If you'd like to see some samples of emails that I have sent you can go to the Resources page on my website; KathrynWheat.com/Resources. You will see a link there for Archived emails.

Whatever system you use, make sure it's not one of those that send out replicated emails to your list. I know many people in the Real Estate market that pay for a service to create emails and send them to their list. As a result, I get the same exact email from several different agents. The only thing that differentiates it from the others is that the email has their picture and name on it. The rest of the content is the same. This makes you look like you lack individuality. I know these email companies charge a lot of money. Don't waste it on something like this. It's like getting a form letter or other junk mail.

It feels like an impersonal template and it is. Make the effort to do your own email. Show your personality. Nobody can do that for you.

Never send emails where everyone can see all the cc (carbon copy) email addresses of everyone on your list. This is close to unforgivable as it shares other people's email address without their permission and is a tremendous invasion of privacy! I've seen people "reply all" to these emails and really rake the sender over the coals for doing this. If you do happen to receive one of these emails and want to reply, don't send your scathing remarks to everyone on the list. It will make you look just as bad as the original sender. When I receive one of these types of emails from someone I personally know, I try to help them out and reply only to the sender and tell them about the email system that I use and let them know that I am available to help them get started if they need me.

I'm going to share with you an email I received from someone that I had met the previous evening at a networking event. No, these aren't typos on my part. This is the actual email that came to me:

"Good Morning Mr. Johnson,

Thank you for the opportunity and taking time to talk to us. It was a pressure meetin you and dissucing each other business. We look forward to seeing you at other events. If you're intersing in our company's services feel free to check our website:"

I remembered the young man that this email supposedly came from. He was a well-spoken gentleman and I suspected that he had not written this email himself. I responded to it and suggested that he check what was being sent out with his name on it. Of course he responded back to me right away apologizing for the email. He was horrified that this email had gone out to Mr. Johnson and to who knows how many people and was so obviously not the kind of impression he wanted to send. If you do decide to hire out and allow someone else to create emails for you, be sure you know what is being sent with your name on it. It's your reputation on the line and your responsibility to take care of it.

When setting up an email template, be sure to include a photo of you. This helps people connect with you and remember you better. Just make sure the photo actually looks like you. No old, overly done photos with big hair and blurry filters! Make sure it's a professional business photo. Consider including a short video. People love video! It's super easy to do even with your phone. You don't have to hire a professional videographer. Don't worry about messing up your words. Just talk normally. Video is much more interesting and personal than flat words on paper. When others can hear your voice inflections, passion, and humor, they will connect with you even better. Three minutes or less is ideal. Just talk about something that's on your mind. Send a holiday greeting or even an invitation to an event. It doesn't have to be anything profound.

When I review the traffic patterns and hits on my website, I can see that some of the most popular videos that I have done are on completely random subjects. One in particular was when I jumped on the Gangnam style dance craze. Two friends and I did a silly rendition of the dance. People thought it was funny because we were just having fun. I actually used it to announce my next networking event. It's just a great way to show your personality. People will feel like they know you.

When you get replies to your emails, make sure to respond and thank the person for their words. If they have questions, answer them. Not many take the time to reply so you should recognize and compliment the ones that take that extra step. This leaves such a great impression in someone's mind. If you use email properly, people will remember your name and what you do. That's what you are working toward!

Here is an example of what staying in touch through email can do for you. When I first started networking, I met a lady named Carol who is an Interior Designer. She allowed me to use one of her blog posts on my website and I added her to my "In List". Five years had passed when she replied to one of my emails asking if we could meet for a cup of coffee. She had seen that I was doing a lot of work with Realtors and wanted to ask me some questions about it. I connected her with some networking opportunities and we began staying in touch more regularly. A few weeks passed by and I received a call from a lady named Kristine who told me that Carol had told her that she should call and talk to me. Kristine was also in need of a way to meet more people in Real Estate. I spent about 45 minutes on the phone with her and began including her on some Real Estate specific invitations. A few more weeks passed by and a lady named Cindy showed up at one of my classes. She had been told that the class was full but she took a chance and came anyway just in case there was a cancellation. It turned out that there was a cancellation and she was able to take a seat in the class. Kristine, whom I still had not met in person, told her that she should meet me. A couple of months after that, Cindy introduced me to James who has subsequently booked me for three of the largest classes that I've taught to date! All of this goes back to that original conversation with Carol over 5 years ago. Had I not put her on my email list and stayed in touch by sending emails that she actually wanted to open, I wouldn't have been able to book these classes with James.

This is a perfect example of how networking works! When you stay in touch with email and don't use it to push your agenda, people will get to know you and be genuinely interested in what you send to them. Remember, you are training someone on whether or not to open your next email every time you hit send. You never know how quickly the relationship will grow. Give it some time. It's not always overnight. Sometimes patience is required!

You may occasionally be asked to share your list with someone, or to promote someone else's business or event. The more well-known you get, the more likely you will be asked to do this. I make it a basic business principal to never share my list. I respect each and every person on my list and would never compromise the integrity of my list by sharing information that those people have trusted me with. I only send out emails with my messages. Just keep this in mind when deciding how you want to treat your list. It's my opinion that your list should never be for sale! If you start sending out promotions for other people, you will get a lot of unsubscribes. People will let you know how they feel about it and it is rarely positive.

"Every company is its own TV station, magazine, and newspaper.

~ Jay Baer

25

Social Media;
is it Worth Your Time?

Social media, if used properly, can be a valuable tool for networking. Just make sure you take the time to fill out all of the information in the bio section and provide your correct contact information for people to reach you. Making your email private defeats the purpose of using social media for business. You must make it easy for people to get in touch with you. If someone tries to connect with me and hasn't taken the time to even put in a photo that tells me something about them. I'm not likely to want to connect with people that look like they do things half way.

Provide links in your email to all of your social media accounts so people can find you and connect with you easily. Mail Chimp provides templates that makes this really easy. Remember, your initial meeting is only the beginning. Social media is another valuable method for keeping the conversation going. After you connect with someone, don't immediately send him or her a sales pitch. That's not what it's for. It's to get to know each other better.

I have done plenty of business through social media connections so don't think it's all just a big time waster. I recently used someone that I know from Twitter to purchase the custom labeled wine that I use for door prizes and other gifting opportunities. We'd been conversing on Twitter for over a year. I went to see them and found that they had a much better deal than I'd had with the previous company that I had been using. This business relationship started all because of Twitter!

Sometimes it can take many months of being casual social media acquaintances before you even get the opportunity, or have a need, to connect on a business level. I "met" one of my biggest sponsors on my website through Twitter. We were connected online only by retweeting and messaging each other for about a year. Then he asked me for information about promoting his business on my website. He's been a returning client for several years.

You can use Facebook, Twitter, YouTube, Pinterest, Instagram, Tumblr, SlideShare, and any other social media sites that might arise as a way for people to get to know who you really are. It's also a great way to learn more about others since postings are usually less filtered than direct conversations at networking functions. People tend to forget the world is watching when posting online updates so you are offered a clearer picture of the real person behind the glowing profile.

Just remember it works both ways. Be mindful of what you post! If you love getting rip roaring drunk on Saturday night, keep that private. Don't use social media as a platform to call people out or to rant. It doesn't look good. If you must vent about something, keep it private and don't blast it all over the web. Share information about networking events that you plan on attending. Invite others to events that you think may interest them. Take photos of people you connect with and post them on your social media sites. This lets people see that you are getting out there and meeting people. Think about sharing interesting articles, videos, quotes or helpful hints. Just stay positive! Like, comment and retweet other people's good thoughts and ideas. It creates good vibes. Don't just use it as a way to be seen. Engage with people. Don't try to sell, sell, sell on social media. People will block your posts or delete you if the only thing they ever see from you is a sales pitch.

Always be respectful of other people's property. By this I mean don't post your stuff on someone else's social media sites without specific permission. It's like putting your sign in someone else's yard. Expect to irritate people and get "un-friended" or "blocked" quickly if you do this. If I accept a friend request and that person immediately posts an ad on my timeline, they are immediately removed from my friends list. Don't use people for their connections. They will see right through it and form undesirable opinions about you. This is not what you are trying to accomplish with networking! Just keep in mind that you aren't there to sell, sell, sell. You are there to start conversations with nice people.

Recently, I was in negotiations with someone regarding my Continuing Education classes. This person went onto my Facebook timeline and posted something along the lines of asking me to reduce my fees. I immediately deleted this post. Social media isn't the place to discuss business negotiations! I learned a lot about this individual from his actions. This was inappropriate and I know that he knew this was a major indiscretion with social media. It made me not want to do business with him at all.

Allow people to see your success, but avoid being all business. It's a bit of a balancing act but its okay to let people see who you are. Social media can work for you, and against you, so remember to be mindful about what you post! If you use social media for business, and you are not a personal trainer, think twice about showing off your new six-pack no matter how hard you have worked to achieve it.

Suggestive or very personal selfies posted on social media may get you tons of "likes" but it doesn't do much for your professional image. People will definitely be talking about you but probably not in a good way. Remember that everything you do contributes to your personal brand and it's up to you to present yourself in the manner that accentuates that brand and doesn't destroy it. Clients will undoubtedly notice the party pics that you post when you've told them you are too busy for a meeting. You don't want questions raised about your honesty and integrity so make sure you are not making conflicting statements.

If you follow these principals and consistently stay in touch with people, you will be remembered. I have had it happen on many occasions where someone approaches me at an event and moves in for a warm greeting. I have no idea who they are because they haven't kept in touch from their end but they feel like they know me because they hear from me on a consistent basis. I just don't know them. So be aware, this may lead to awkward hugs from strangers.

One more small word of caution: Once you become a networking guru, people may try to capitalize on your notoriety. It's always good to give first when it comes to networking. I wholeheartedly believe in this philosophy. Just make sure you aren't the only one giving. If that is the case, you are being used and you need to learn to say "no". You can't take care of everyone else if you aren't taking care of yourself. Don't allow others to take advantage of your kindness if it's a detriment to you.

One time I "won" a prize. I use the quotations here because it became obvious that it was a ploy. You may think, so what if it was a ploy, you won! But the prize was an entrance ticket to a conference that was struggling to sell tickets. Initially I was thrilled to win. Then I found that this prize was given to me with a set of instructions on how to publicly thank the giver of said prize on social media with photos. I felt used and insulted by their tactics and ended up declining the prize. It made me very disappointed in the person who was doing this because had they not dictated how I should thank them, I probably would have actually done even more than what they demanded. So beware of 'friends' bearing gifts!

"A life spent making
mistakes is not only
more honorable,
but more useful
than a life spent
doing nothing.

~ George Bernard Shaw

26

When You Get
Off Track

Occasionally you may get off track and your networking efforts may get derailed. You may have changed companies, or careers, or the business you previously had went down the tubes. Perhaps you got busy with work concerns and special projects or you've been networking in different areas than normal. Before you know it, weeks or even months pass by without you making it to your regular networking meetings and you feel as if you've lost touch. In addition to that, you haven't been sending out emails to your contacts and have neglected to keep people updated through social media. It feels like starting over! But don't worry; sometimes we do have to start over. It's really not the worst thing that can happen to you. Don't be afraid of getting back out there. You can start over if you have to. Some of the most successful entrepreneurs failed many times before they found that one idea that blew up to be a huge success so you aren't alone.

I've heard stories of innumerable mistakes people have made when networking. Whatever your story is, you can recover from past mistakes or missteps. Past regrettable choices or decisions are not excuses to give up on networking. No matter what you may have messed up, it is recoverable. When I was a little girl and I got into trouble, I was taught to apologize for my mistakes. I really wanted to come up with viable excuses as to why I'd behaved so badly and I would say, "Yeah, but I didn't know it was bad", or whatever excuse I could come up with to try and justify my behavior. A sincere apology is never followed by an excuse. If you mess up, just apologize and move on. My grandmother decided I needed to stop making excuses and just apologize so she would insist that I apologize without any "yeah buts". That works well for adults too. So no "yeah buts" allowed! No excuses are good enough to not give it another go. You can re-enter the networking world no matter the circumstance.

Even if you had a relationship with the host of a popular networking group, and it went south, don't let it stop you from getting back out there. So what if you have to see your ex when you attend these meetings? Just return to the group and behave in a professional manner. Hold your head high and others will respect you for it.

Maybe you got into a battle with a competitor and didn't behave professionally. You won't be the first person who has had to overcome this type of problem. We have all made mistakes. I know some of them can seem insurmountable. But they aren't. Push past your discomfort. Once you take the first step to return, you will see that most people are forgiving, especially if they see you sincerely trying to make positive changes. The more genuine and honest you are about what happened, the more willing people will be to accept your earnest apology. Just be authentic. None of us are perfect.

If you have neglected your email list and it's been several months since you've sent an email, you will need to use the first email to let people know you are back. Then tell them where you've been and give some sort of explanation. It's important to address the elephant in the room, don't just ignore it. Perhaps even use the subject line,

"I'm back!" The main thing is to not let any more time pass before you get going again. You can even utilize social media platforms to announce your return to networking. Ask questions about where people are meeting and what new groups may have been formed. People love to help so don't be shy about asking for updates on networking.

The best thing to do is to jump back in and return to the networking scene as soon as you can. Whether you are starting a brand new venture or you inherited a 50-year-old business, you must get back into it and go start some conversations. Just remember to be authentic. You can start with implementing the principals that I've outlined in this book. It will set you ahead of most people because now you are equipped with the knowledge needed to turn things around and make networking a productive method for growing your business. There will be some new faces, and some familiar ones, but you will get back into the swing of meeting people again quickly, especially if you had previously made strong connections. People will be glad to see you return. Be prepared to answer questions from your old connections about where you've been and what happened, especially if you haven't stayed in touch at all. If there was drama attached to your temporary exit from the scene, steer clear of new drama that others may want to drum up. Make apologies if necessary and move on. Rise above the drama and remain professional. Just go start some conversations!

---◦◦◦---

"Whatever you can do, or dream you can, begin it."

~ Johann Wolfgang von Goeth

---◦◦◦---

27

You are
Ready!

Whether you are an individual proprietor, entrepreneur, or part of a large corporation, you should now understand the necessity of networking to build your circle of influence within your industry and how having that large circle of influence can positively impact you and your company. I advised you at the beginning of this book, that what I teach is most likely different from anything you've been told before. That's what makes it so effective. It allows you to be you.

People want to know who you are before they will care what you do. Don't go out networking and put on a "business face". Of course you need to be professional and be cognizant of the fact that you are conducting business, but people want to know the real you and not some actor in a movie. Forget the script that you think people are waiting to hear. Show up as yourself. Be you. People will notice your authenticity and genuine approach and this will build trust in you first, and then that trust will transfer to what you have to offer.

So many people are out there trying to sell to anyone that crosses their path. If you adopt the mindset that you need to begin with starting a conversation with no destination in mind then you'll be leaps and bounds ahead of everyone one else trying to push their agenda on everyone they meet. People will notice that your approach is not one of someone desperately trying to sell, but one of such confidence in your product or service that you don't need to constantly push it.

The days are here where having an established online reputation is vital. Creating a personal brand is essential to growing your reputation. Registering your name as a dot com is the first step to establishing a recognized brand. Once you have decided what your brand name is, put it on everything you do and make sure you stay consistent with the name you register. People want evidence that you have made a good name for yourself and that you are a respected business person in your field. When someone is considering doing business with you they will search for information about you on the Internet and it's up to you to provide them with accurate and positive evidence of your expertise and experience.

Carry business cards with you and make sure they convey stability. You never know where you'll have an opportunity to network so keep cards in your car, wallet, or purse. Use good stock paper and include a recent photo so people can easily remember you. We give out our business cards so people will have easy access to our contact information. Make sure your card is clutter free and easy to read. If it's effortless for people to contact you, they are much more likely to do so.

Create an irresistible introduction. Prepare a way to introduce yourself that is natural. Don't ever try to "pitch" when networking. Pitching your product or service upon meeting someone for the first time turns people off faster than you can say, "Buy my stuff". Instead, start conversations and get to know people. Allow them to get to know you. Yes, let people know what you do but remember, what you do isn't the only thing that defines you. You are so much more than that! Letting people see the rest of the story will allow them to decide if you are someone that they want to connect with.

In this book, I've outlined proper networking protocol and etiquette so you know what makes a good first impression. Make a statement when you walk into a room by dressing professionally. When you make the effort to get out there and take the initiative you must make the best first impression possible to ensure those efforts aren't wasted. This means pay attention to the details because other people will be making quick judgments about you based on your appearance. And of course, don't forget to wear your nametag to help people remember your name.

In any situation, good manners are necessary. Being polite and respectful will make you stand out in a positive way. How you greet people, how you eat, and the topics of conversation that you engage in, all say something about you as a person. You never know who is watching you from afar. Once you create a habit of practicing good manners and respecting other people, you will never have to worry about who is watching you. Showing respect for others is always the right choice.

Try out several different types of networking groups and events. Most will let you visit a couple of times before you must make a commitment to join. There will certainly be some that you love and some that you can't wait to end. When you visit a group for the first time, walk in with a smile. It will help you look and feel more confident. Before you attend a new meeting, try to talk to the host or someone that is a member of that group and ask questions about the structure and focus of that particular group. This will help you determine which groups are the right fit for you before you go. If you decide to join a group that has fees, make sure you take a look at the entire picture. Don't network yourself out of business.

Remember that you can network anywhere! It doesn't have to be in an organized networking group. Take advantage of meeting people everywhere you go. It can be the gym, golf course, charitable fundraisers, community events, bunko group or anywhere you see people on a regular basis and get to know them. By the same token, always remember that people are watching and observing what kind of person you are at all times, not just when you want them to. This is why you absolutely must be authentic because if you are not, they will catch you being yourself at some point and will wonder what kind of person you really are.

When you are at an event, remember; don't lead with your card. Talk with people first. You won't connect with everyone and that's okay. When you start meeting people, don't pitch your business right off. Instead, introduce yourself; let them get to know about you as you get to know them. Let a relationship grow and develop naturally. The idea is to just go start some conversations and then see where they lead. Listen more than you talk. Ask people about themselves. Pay attention to their body language and make sure you are conscious of your own. Be confident and approachable.

You must find a way to stand out in a sea of networkers and one of the best ways is to become a speaker. I understand that is a scary concept for many people as it was for me, but when you speak, you establish yourself as an expert. It allows you to get in front of a room full of people who will get to know you even better so it's a great way to leverage your time. You could never meet everyone in the room at a crowded networking event but if you are the speaker, everyone will know you. Start with small crowds and short speeches and you will see that it gets easier each time and your confidence will grow. Invest in yourself by hiring a speaking coach or consultant if that's what you need to get started.

Most importantly, don't let all the business cards you collect gather dust on your desk. Get organized with how you stay in touch with people so you can continue the conversations that you started while networking. This last step is often overlooked and it's where many people fail. All of the networking you do is a waste of time if you miss this part. Unfortunately, we are soon forgotten if we skip this. Stay in touch! Take action and schedule follow up meetings with the people that you immediately connect with. Utilize social media, send cards, and build an email list to add value to people's lives. Engage in conversations through email and social media. People won't forget you if you stay in touch.

Don't ever jump into a sales pitch when you are following up after your initial meeting. Remember, when you were out networking, you started a bunch of conversations with no destination in mind. The same principal applies to how you handle future conversations. By this time, the people you are meeting with already know what you do. You don't have to push your services. People will respect you more if you don't pressure them into listening to your presentation or pitch. I guarantee you they will let you know if they need your service. If you respect them, they will appreciate that. The best thing that can happen is that they will go around telling others all about you and how much they admire and respect the way you do business. It's much better to have hundreds of people out there saying great things about you than it is to get that one sale you pressured someone into. So relax, it takes time for productive business relationships to develop.

Ronald began using these principals with networking five years ago and has built his lucrative Personal Branding business entirely through networking. Over the years, he has been able to consistently increase the cost of the systems that he sells and reach a new level of prospects. Every week he has people call him and tell him that they got his name from someone who said that they needed to talk to him. About 75% of these referrals turn into sales. It's because he has built a loyal tribe of people that are out there saying great things about his business and leading prospects to him. When that happens, you don't have to sell anything. People come to you ready to buy.

Maritza contacted me a few months ago to tell me that she was so proud that she had implemented all that she had learned about how to properly network and how it has helped her grow her Home Staging business. She's set up a website landing page, sends regular emails and starts lots of conversations. She has even stepped outside of her comfort zone and started speaking and teaching classes on Home Staging and her business has taken off. A year ago she was just getting started. Now she has a steady stream of income from Home Staging.

Barbara needed to give a short presentation on a topic that she was very passionate about. She understood the importance of sharing her information to make a difference in other peoples lives and aspired to do well. After writing and memorizing her speech, she was still a bundle of nerves until she called me for help. I helped her with some simple body language and relaxation techniques for speakers. Then I reminded her of the most important thing and that was to be herself and let her passion show. That is what people would remember! She was thrilled that she was able to confidently give an effective presentation.

After a recent class for an ABWA (American Business Women's Association) group titled, "How to Create the Perfect Introduction", I received a letter from the chapter president telling me she loved my energy and seeing the members interact with me. She also told me how everyone was implementing the tips and techniques that I had taught and as a result, their introductions were so much more interesting and fun to listen to.

After I helped Ryan update his Social Media profiles and set up MailChimp to send interesting email campaigns, he quickly saw how the combination of the two led to his increased recognition as an expert in his field and significantly improved his presence on the Internet.

Sharon was unsure of how to engage with people at networking events until I shared with her some of my simple but effective approaches. Now she no longer feels anxiety when entering a room full of people because she has a plan that she knows will work.

I recently heard a remark from a student in one of my classes that this was the first course that she'd ever taken that actually told her not to sell! She said it was such a relief to hear that her instincts were right all along. She had been so uncomfortable with the way she was approaching networking that she dreaded attending events. She was really excited about trying out the techniques that I teach. Once she implemented those ideas, she said that it felt completely natural and could already tell that people were drawn to her simply because her approach was now one of authenticity and fun. Instead of people running from her, they were connecting with her and wanted to get to know her better.

Now that you understand the concept of how to Network Naked, you are ready to join any networking group knowing that you have the knowledge and skills needed to approach business professionals in a networking environment with confidence and poise. It's time to give it a shot! When you put into practice all that you have learned from this book, as many others have done, you will see how people react to you better than ever before. They will naturally let their guard down and real business deals will materialize because of the new trust and comfort people will experience when they are around you.

Remember, this is a journey that I have been on too. These principles are what I've used to build a lucrative speaking and consulting business and I'm confident that I can help you do the same. If you've always wanted to become a confident public speaker, get your nervous jitters under control, make a memorable first impression, be great at giving an irresistible introduction that people will really listen to, or simply become more comfortable at networking, reach out to me through my website, KathrynWheat. com. I'd be honored to provide consulting and mentoring using my simple but effective methods so you can be more composed, relaxed and confident. I want to help you put into practice all that I have learned so you will thrive!

Significant business connections are out there waiting to be made. You can't afford to not be part of the business conversations that are going on. You can be one of the people who have learned to make networking work for you. But the most important thing is to just get started now with all that you have learned and, remember, have fun and #NetworkNaked!

Now, go start some conversations!

Connect with me through my website at: **KathrynWheat.com**

CPSIA information can be obtained
at www.ICGtesting.com
Printed in the USA
FFOW03n1826141117
43458342-42126FF